# Branding your
# Job Search

## Achieving Career Goals with your Next Job

**Michael Glinter**

**Branding Success LLC**

http://www.brandingsuccessllc.com

ISBN 978-0-578-09703-9

# ACKNOWLEDGEMENTS

I want to dedicate this book to all the people in my life that supported me through the years in my endeavors of becoming a success in the recruiting business. I especially want to thank the people that pushed me to write this book. To my spouse, my friends, my coworkers, and many of the candidates that I worked with – Thank You. Thank you for giving me the courage, the desire, and the fulfillment of being able to pass along my knowledge to those that could use it. Special thanks to Andrew for supporting me through this project, and Bill for bringing me on to be a part of the team. Also, thanks goes to George, Sonnie, and Kristin for helping me bring the most to people in their career goals and job search.

# CONTENTS

# PREFACE

When I think of the phrases and quotes that have motivated me throughout my career, the one that has influenced my decisions the most is "knowledge is power." This phrase is the inspiration for this book. After 12 years of being the most successful recruiters in our company and one of the top in the country, and placing well over 1,500 candidates in top management and executive positions throughout the nation, I've gathered insight by virtue of my unique position in working with companies and candidates in the role of recruiter. My desire in publishing this book is to educate the general public in what it takes to qualify themselves for better employment and achieve their long term career goals. I have created the company Branding Success, LLC (http://www.brandingsuccessllc.com) to help drive change in people's lives through personal fulfillment and increased income, redirect their lives to attain their career goals, and ultimately help companies and managers brand initiatives to create success within their institutions.

Over the past two years, as the recession settled in and the unemployment rate rose, a trend started to emerge: the longer people were unemployed, the more desperate they became. Desperate people, unfortunately, behave in ways that inhibit their ability to gain employment and further their careers.

For years I have counseled, coached, lead, taught, mentored, and prepared potential applicants through the process of interviewing for career positions. I often think that nothing in the recruitment business could surprise me. But I'm constantly surprised and frustrated by some candidates' behavior; they really don't understand that simple mistakes and poor decisions can cost them the job they have worked so hard to get. It is because of this frustration that I decided to put this book out there to help people in not only the simple changes, but also how they could brand themselves for the future.

This book is designed to help you in many different ways.

- Identifying Career Goals
- Finding Fulfillment in your Career
- Developing the best way to Represent yourself on Paper
- Marketing yourself to an Organization
- Identifying the right Industries and Companies to Target
- Using Recruiters as Resources
- Taking advantage of Technology and Social Networking
- Preparing for Phone and Face-to-Face Interviews
- Asking the right Questions
- Getting the Offer you Want
- Making the new Position work for your Career

Most importantly it is designed to help you create an image, a brand that represents you, and to give you the capability of standing out above your competition.

## Purpose

As you read this book you will better understand the purpose and process of a job search. As one better understands components of the job search, he or she is better able to succeed in reaching the end goal. For many, the long-term goal may be to become employed. For others, the goal might be to improve their employment. But regardless of your current employment status, this book will help you create objectives and strategies for reaching your long-term goal.

## Building a Resume

How you present yourself to possible employers on paper establishes the foundation for the rest of the process. The resume is the key that opens the door of success. But if a resume is weak, you will not likely succeed.

Additionally, as you work through the process to create a strong resume, you will simultaneously establish a brand that represents you individually.

## Branding

You must first understand your marketing and branding power, which is, in my experience, both the most important and most overlooked factor when a candidate presents him or herself to potential employers. When you turn yourself into a brand, potential employers are able to associate your skills and experience with the overall success of the company.

## Driving Change through Branding

When you brand yourself in a way that distinguishes you from others, you are driving the change that is necessary for you to be viewed as successful. Branding your skills and your experiences can also help companies understand the value that you bring to the company in the long-term. Value has become one of the most important things that companies consider when keeping and growing employees with their organization.

## Technical Advantages

Over the years, technology has changed the way candidates seek out job opportunities and make connections with companies. The job market has changed drastically within the past ten years as technology has advanced. Most people don't use technology effectively. When I first started in this business back in 1999, the job search consisted of searching newspapers and waiting by fax machines for a receipt. Today, a candidate searches the internet and can send a hundred resumes in an hour. The exciting part of the internet and technology, such as social networking, is its capacity to improve candidates' ability to brand themselves to companies.

## Interviewing Techniques

Interviewing is an art in itself. It's crucial that you understand how your behaviors are perceived during phone and face-to-face interviews. This book will discuss what your mannerisms communicate to an interviewer, how your words and tone inform an interviewer's opinion of you, and how your body language, behavior, and speech build you into a powerful brand.

## Getting the Job you Want

When a candidate is unemployed or underemployed, there is a significant temptation to accept whatever position comes along, but the position should be a strategic step higher on the ladder toward the long-term goal. Even small steps in the right direction are better than steps in the wrong direction. This book will help you discern which positions you ought to consider, how to pursue those positions, and how to professionally negotiate the employment offer. Successfully navigating these steps toward gainful employment will depend on your understanding of the company. This book will discuss how to properly research a company to ensure you are in the ideal situation to meet with success.

## Assessing your New Job

Once you have transitioned into a new job and have had time to settle in, it's important that you assess the current situation compared to the long-term goal. This is an appropriate time to review long-term career goals and aspirations and ensure this job is a step forward in that plan.

My hope is that when you are done reading this book, you can truly improve your approach to your search. Branding who you are within the industry to the companies you work for will help you immediately grow your abilities to attaining your career goals. Find the opportunity and meet the goals of where you want to go in your career. This will ultimately lead to the one thing that everyone wants in a job and a career: fulfillment.

# ESTABLISHING CAREER GOALS

Tim was recently laid off from his job and he knows the economy is not good at all. He also knows that after twenty years of being with the same company, he is going to have significant obstacles with this job search because he does not having a college education. While being with the same company for twenty years was a great benefit, he is realizing that he never made a long-term career plan for what he wanted to accomplish. He also has never put down on paper who he was or what he did, so writing a resume from scratch will be a challenge.

Samantha is currently a Senior Marketing Manager for an energy company in the Midwest. She took this job three years ago thinking that it would be a good move for her career, but she is not happy with the work, industry, or direction in which she feels her career is heading. She does not want to keep changing jobs, but she does not feel confident that a new job would be any more fulfilling.

George has been unemployed for eight months and is running out of time. He needs to find a job but no one wants to talk to him because of his previous work titles and level of experience, combined with the money he has customarily made in the past. Everyone he talks to feels as if he is overqualified, that he might be taking the position just till he finds something better, or that he was making way too much money in the past and is not going to be happy at the level the company wishes to pay him.

Pete just graduated college. He is so excited that he finally completed his degree in Psychology but has no idea what he wants to do with it or how to approach writing a resume and interviewing. His parents paid his way through school so this will be his very first job in the real world. Other than odd jobs here and there, the only true experience he has is in leadership and participation in classes and groups in school.

Here you have four people in totally different situations and places in their life. They really do not have a lot in common, but they do have one important thing that links them together. All four have to figure out how to proceed in life in finding fulfillment in their careers and how they market themselves to companies.

The first step in starting your job search is setting goals that will govern how you will pursue your next job. Everything you do has to have end goals. Career goals can come from a job search, a conversation, an interaction with a peer, or a discussion with a relative. In this chapter, you will learn the things you need to consider in order to create goals for your job search, both short-term and long-term. These goals will then help you formulate a plan for how you want to actually perform the job search specific to your needs.

Establishing these career goals is a journey to reach the point of ultimate fulfillment in your life. That fulfillment can be defined in many ways and is not the same for everyone. Achieving ultimate fulfillment in your career can only be attainable if you dream big and take the necessary steps to get there.

It is extremely important that the initial goals you set focus on are the things that make you happy and allow you to feel like you are gaining a level of achievement. Try to make goals that excite you and that will, when achieved, give you a sense of fulfillment. Try to identify as many of these goals that give you these feelings now when you are in the initial planning stages so you only have to tweak your goals and plan down the road.

Defining Fulfillment

Think about what types of responsibilities and objectives you have in your current or most recent job and how you can apply these to the goals of your career. These should be the basis of how you market yourself. Think about the things missing in your job that will ultimately help you attain this goal. By identifying what is missing, you are creating the framework of what is valued in your job search.

Start by thinking back to when you were a child. What were your goals and feelings back then as you imagined your future? Then consider how those feelings have changed or were altered because of significant life events such as going to college, getting married, buying your first house, etc. Evaluate how these changes affected your feelings and direction in life. You will likely find that some of these events were only significant for a short period of time while others have proven to be a powerful force that continues to drive you toward achieving your goals.

Now think about your career aspirations today. How have your aspirations changed? What about your career is not changing and ultimately is preventing you from being happy in your career? This is the basis and the foundation for the long-term fulfillment that you are looking for.

Another thing to consider when thinking about your ultimate long term goals is to look at the environmental and personal factors that have shaped the way your life has been up to this point. Often times, outside, uncontrollable factors can seriously change the direction you are going even though it is not the direction you want to be in. Unemployment is the most common uncontrollable factor that creates a person's need to find a new job. Since you are going through this exercise today, I can assume that when you look back on your career path you are not completely satisfied. Take ownership of what you feel is ultimately going to bring that long-term fulfillment and do not let this go. That could mean taking ownership of failures of decisions you have made in the past and use that toward doing better for the future, or deciding what motivates you in achieving your long term goals and using these motivations to overcome challenges getting to them. No two people travel the same career path to get to the same position or end goal. This is where flexibility in your career goals and job search become important.

Creating Career Goals

Take what you have learned about yourself and your life up to this point as learning experiences that has assisted you in creating your life goals. Don't reflect on your past experiences as bad decisions, but more so experimentation in life. Now that you have gone through these experiments, how does this impact your overall feeling toward reaching your goals?

You definitely need to have the realization that you may have to take giant steps back in life to get back on the right path. You need to accept this. Do not take this as a negative because the end result is still the same. Most people feel that if they take steps back in their career and in life that it is a poor reflection on them. As long as you can justify these changes then you ultimately will win.

A great example of a person taking two steps forward and one step backward is my father, Paul Glinter. He was a very dedicated man when it came to his job, who, for more than 25 years, worked for the same company and worked his way up to become one of the senior leaders within the organization. My father was paid very well and reaped the many benefits from his efforts to be promoted in his career. Then one day he walked into his office to find a manila envelope on his desk. He knew that several months prior, the company had been sold to a private equity company and he had been expecting some major changes. But knowing he was a valued employee because that had done so much for the organization, he never thought that any of the changes would negatively impact him. Unfortunately, when he opened the envelope he learned he had lost his job.

At the time my father lost his job, he was in his mid-fifties. He was established in his local community and emotionally connected with life-long friends; he really didn't want to uproot his entire life. His resume showed he lacked major qualifications in order to be competitive, specifically a four-year degree, which disqualified him from many jobs. He knew he was going to be challenged by this search, but he decided to be creative about how he approached it. Many of the concepts and thoughts expressed in this book drove what he did next.

After several months of unsuccessful searching, my father decided to work with a career counseling service offered by the company that laid him off. They helped him answer the following question for himself: "Was there anything you always wanted to do but didn't because of your career with company ABC?" After a considerable amount of thought, he concluded he really did have aspirations that he never pursued. My father always wanted to get involved in architectural drafting (AutoCAD) and use some of his skills he acquired during his military service. He had never seriously considered pursuing anything in this line of business because he had already started moving forward in his career and found it to be extremely gratifying at the time. But another question he had never made himself answer while employed by the company that laid him off was, "Do I feel fulfilled?"

So my father went back to school. He enrolled in a local technical college near his home to pursue further training and certifications in architecture. After a year of tireless studying and work, he completed the first step to the next phase of his life and possible fulfillment: my father landed a job with a privately-held, local architectural firm and spent seven wonderful years with the company before his retirement. I recall the many times I saw my father when he came home from work after working a long 10-12 hour day at the architecture firm. He always seemed to be happy. He always had a smile on his face. I could tell by his physical appearance that he started to feel a level of satisfaction that he had not experienced in his previous job.

One of the most fundamental lessons my father's story teaches us is that he used up 25 years of his life to finally realize that what he was doing was not making him happy. He took a ¾ cut in pay in his salary to pursue a dream that would ultimately lead him to the one thing that he never had personally achieved: true fulfillment.

What is the most important thing to you in your career?
- Attaining a higher level or new type of position
- How much you are making
- Your commute or desire to change locations
- Type of work that you are currently doing
- Work environment

These all contribute toward the ultimate goal when performing your search. So make sure you take note of these things. Most importantly, write it down! You cannot create a goal without documenting it. You have to have a reminder on why you are searching. Create a list or a chart that you can check off when entertaining a new position or new role to make sure it gets you what you are looking to achieve. It doesn't have to be a list of just your primary goals, but you can have secondary goals as well. Just because you want to move to a new city or state doesn't mean you want to move into a dead-end job that doesn't challenge or fulfill you in the long-term.

When you are writing down your primary and secondary goals, do not be afraid to dream and think big. It shouldn't concern you how you are going to achieve your goals, but more so what you want to achieve. Think about what you want for yourself and where do you want your career to go long term. Think about what aspects of your personality, your life, and your abilities you want to draw from when getting to this point in your life. Think about what will make you happy. Understand that anything you write down, like everything else in your career goals, is subject to change, so nothing you write down is stupid. It's simply the way you are thinking at the time. Do not be afraid of putting down too many ideas or ideas that seem to conflict with each other. For example, you might have a goal to play music but you also want to own your own business. These are two distinct ideas and two distinct positions in life. You may or may not be able to get to these two positions in your life at the same time, but you can bring them together. Think of the outcome – you could have a music store and offer classes on writing and playing music. You could also own your own recording studio and help others write music while you play and create your own music.

Often times, people decide to delete ideas, dreams, and aspirations from their life-long plan because they cannot envision themselves ever being able to tie the two together. Do not worry about this today. The thing you need to worry about today is what will bring the long-term fulfillment that you desire.

You should have short-term and long-term goals. Make sure your goals are realistic. You cannot expect a company to hire you to be its Chief Executive Officer if you have been an administrative assistant for the last ten years. This is why both short- and long-term goals are necessary. It's a great long-term goal to be the CEO of a company, but it is not a short term goal, especially if you first have to obtain experience or education to qualify for a position. Focusing on each short-term goal will eventually lead you to accomplishing your long-term goals.

Learn to not dismiss an opportunity too quickly. The easiest response is "I am not interested." But do you really know your level of interest? Have you gained enough information about the opportunity to determine whether or not it will help or not help you achieve your goals? The biggest mistake most candidates make is they make decisive decisions without proper information to determine the direction of their search. When entertaining a job opportunity, remind yourself of your short- and long-term goals and how a specific opportunity will affect your career. Utilize the lists you have made to help you determine this. Do not just dismiss information; utilize it.

Don't forget that your career goals can change. Nothing you write down or identify as important to you is ever permanent unless you make that a permanent part of your life. You need to have flexibility in life plan and be willing to take risks and make changes to make it to where you want to be.

Creating a list of Career Expectations

Create a list of what you want to have in your career and job as well as what you do not want. Again, record it. Write down things you expect and do not expect to be apart of your day-to-day job requirements, but make sure you are realistic. For example, if you are working in the Food Service, Manufacturing, or Emergency Medical industries, it is not realistic to believe you will have a normal, nine-to-five workday. Determine these ideals based on the type of work you do and the industry or field you are in.

If you are married, or there are other people in your life that will be affected by your goals and job changes, make sure you communicate and discuss these goals with these people. Even though they will not ultimately make the decision concerning your goals becoming reality, your relationship with these people may change in the pursuit of your goals. Understand what those changes might be. Some of the things that will affect your spouse or family are work hours and schedule, relocation, and work-family balance.

Finding a position that will bring you fulfillment is not the only goal to have. You also need to determine what you expect in a company you work for. Create a wish list of the things you need in a company and things you want in a company and use this to evaluate the companies in your search. As we will discuss later in this book, you should also utilize this list when interviewing the company.

In 2010, unemployment was the primary reason that drove people to actively search in the job market. Unemployment can distract us from long-term goals because the short-term, immediate, sometimes desperate need for money drives our focus toward survival. It is okay for you to accept the fact that your short-term goal may not ultimately allow you to achieve your long-term goal, but try to look at the big picture. You can look at a career change or a job as simply a "job" that makes you money, or you can look at it as an opportunity to get your "career" going in the direction you want it to go in. Often times these short-term goal fulfillments could also change the way you look at your long-term goals. Do not let unemployment detract from your beliefs on the type of environment or company you want to work for. For example, if you do not feel you can be happy in an environment where you are micromanaged, accepting a job in a highly autocratic management environment will not help you stay in a job for a longer period of time, and certainly will not create a successful relationship between you and your employer.

One of the most effective approaches is to focus on what added goals you can bring to add value or a solution to a company. When a company is doing a search for an employee, they too have a goal or need that they are trying to fulfill. Therefore, by making one of your goals to help a company create a solution for a problem or meet an existing need will ultimately create a win-win for both parties. Remember that companies are evaluating and measuring how each decision they make affects whether the organizations are profitable. One of your tasks is to help them feel confident in your ability to make them profitable. How will you, as a new hire, affect the costs, the effectiveness, the efficiency, and the trends related to a company's bottom line? While companies definitely do care about their employees' goals, short-term and long-term, they have goals, too.

Achieving your short-term and long-term goals involves creating successful relationships between yourself and the people that will help you succeed. Remember that every person with whom you interact that is involved in your career or job search could substantially help you toward your goals Do not close any doors. Even though the person you're speaking to today cannot help you with your immediate needs, that person might be able to help you with your long-term goals. Allowing a disconnect between yourself and a potential employer will negatively affect your abilities to accomplish any goal you have in your career.

Once you have established your short-term and long-term goals, you have to remember that you need to create value for the other party so that they have an interest in helping you achieve your goal. To illustrate, a person should not visit a used car lot and expect the sales person to take a loss on the vehicle. Your goal (to save money on a car) is not going to benefit the sales person. You need to make sure that whatever your goals are, they bring some type of value to the other party that you are working with. This can be used not only in your job search, but this can be used in all areas of your life. Make your goal of the situation, search, conversation, confrontation, or activity such that it focuses on the company's needs as well as your own.

## Sharing your Goals

Take your list to other people in your life and talk to them about your life-long aspirations and future desires. Try to find people that you know are going to be objective in their thinking and who will be honest with you. I often think about the man who lived next door to my family while I was growing up; he was relentless about becoming a singer. He had an awful voice yet he still kept trying to get into the music industry. No one had the mindset or the guts to tell him that he did not have a voice for singing but that there were other careers within the music industry besides that of a vocal performer. Unfortunately, no one was willing or able to tell him this.

It is very important to get honest feedback from the people who want to see you succeed. Those who have known you longer are more likely to give you honest and accurate opinions about your skills and talents. These people have seen how you have grown and how you have matured in your life. These people have seen you pursue goals and how you've handled success and failure. These people offer an outsider's perspective of what you realistically may be able to achieve.

## Evaluating your Plan

Now that you have had people look at your plan and your goals for your career, take some time to sit down and evaluate whether your goals are realistic. It is not only important that your goals are attainable, but that your goals align with the aspects of your life that make you who you are. To illustrate, if one of your goals is that you want to be an Aerospace Engineer but you have terrible analytical and mathematical skills, you should probably re-evaluate that goal. It is not realistic for someone who lacks such technical skills to be able to succeed in such a highly technical job.

Evaluating your skills will help you measure your ability to be successful. Your skills may be of a technical, leadership, communication, or physical nature. They may range from being able to type 70 wpm, speak a second language, manage large corporate teams, or to run a marathon. Write down the skills in which you are very strong and the skills in which you are moderately strong. Now, while considering your goals, identify which of your skills will be necessary to accomplish your goals. Do you already have most of the skills that will help you accomplish your goals? Which skills do you lack for success in achieving your goals? Are you able to acquire and/or improve these necessary skills? If you find yourself missing skills that are crucial to be successful in your short- and long-term goals, and you aren't able to get them through education or training, you may need to re-evaluate your goals.

Personality can also play a very important role in your ability to accomplish things in life. A great example would be if one of your goals is to be a TV spokesperson for a large company or brand, but you are deathly afraid of public speaking, then that may be a problem. It is very difficult for a person to objectively evaluate his or her own personality. There are various tests available that can help identify strengths and weaknesses of your personality. I recommend the Myers-Briggs personality test. This test will help you better understand your personality's strengths and weaknesses, how others perceive your personality, and which careers are most compatible with your personality descriptors.

Lastly, it is important for you to look at your professional and personal interests in life. Also consider how people have influenced these things in your life. The best way to do this is to look back at your life and think about the people, events, and beliefs that have impacted you the most. This exercise is usually a combination of positive and negative memories and feelings. This helps defined what things you enjoy doing and what you do not enjoy doing. Understanding what truly interests you in life creates a positive energy and will help you achieve your long-term goals.

Your current job, that of a job candidate, seems to require substantial time and effort. Remember that the most worthy goals should require the most and best of a person. Now is the time to take control of your future by planning, working, evaluating, and planning again. If your long-term goals are worthwhile, the preparation and work required to succeed will be worth the investment. This is where building yourself into a brand becomes most effective and starts taking shape.

Tim, at this stage, realizes he needs to come up with ideas on how he could feel accomplished in his life. He starts to write down all of his career achievements that made him feel rewarded along with bringing value to the company. He uses this information to build his resume from a template listing his accomplishments and the success he had in the past. Knowing that he enjoyed the type of work he did as a senior level manager in the manufacturing industry, he doesn't want to change the direction of his career, but he does have to change his approach for getting himself noticed by companies. He decides his short-term goal is to be hired by a company at least in a first- or second-level management role, and his long-term goal is to continue to work his way up within the company, hopefully leading to an equity position.

Samantha has realized that even though she loves marketing, she just does not feel she can apply her skills in the energy industry. She also really loves working with brands instead of general company marketing. She finds a lot of fulfillment in building a brand and being responsible for creating a brand that is memorable to consumers. She wants to one day be an executive over a large-scale international brand. She has decided that her short-term goal is to be hired by a consumer products company in some type of marketing or brand management role and work her way up to the executive level of a well-known brand.

George has been in the finance business for 32 years. His last position was that of CEO of a finance investment company. He has been applying for all types of positions, from Finance Manager at a localized branch all the way up to the CEO of a finance organization. Time is ticking and he can't seem to get anyone to take him seriously. His long-term goals have always been to help people grow the values of their portfolios, so George has decided to look at the big picture. He starts considering other types of finance and creditor-type roles where he can still work with consumers, but more so as a company, and help them grow money. He realizes he has to reposition his resume and the way he presents himself to future employers. Although his long-term goals are fairly vague because he feels fulfilled in helping companies being more financial rewarded, his short-term goal is simple – get a position in a role that somehow deals with company spending, savings, or investments.

Although Pete's academic performance was at the top of his class, he really does not know what he wants to do. The one thing he keeps thinking about is how much he loves working with people. So he decides the most rewarding type of business would be working in the service industry. However, he wants to try to encompass his education in his day-to-day occupation. Pete decides to pursue a position that would involve some type of counseling, coaching, people development, or any other type of avenues where he can work to improve how people feel about themselves, find self-worth, and achieve fulfillment in their lives. His long-term goal would be either to run his own family counseling practice, work with non-profits in community involvement roles, or be an athletic coach or personal health trainer. He realizes that in order for him to get to his long-term goal he needs to pick an industry or company that specializes in this type of field or that will help get him the initial foundation of experience needed to get to his long-term goals.

# DEFINING YOUR JOB SEARCH

One of the biggest decisions you need to make in defining your job search is whether you are looking for full-time, part-time, or temporary employment. This is going to dramatically affect how you approach communicating with companies, applying for jobs, and investigating positions that fulfill your goals that you have created. All three types of employment can be effective to working toward career goals that you have identified. When working toward a career goal, it is not necessarily about jumping both feet first, but attacking the goal one step at a time – sometimes the steps can be significant and require you to move beyond your comfort zone, and sometimes they can be gradual and almost effortless.

## Full- / Part-time Employment

The common difference between full-time and part-time jobs is that full-time jobs typically target a person's long-term goals and skills, whereas part-time positions often are used to help supplement income or time. People frequently use part-time jobs when they are trying to change the direction of their career or assist in re-targeting goals that they have missed in their current job.

For me, writing this book and working as a consultant is a part-time position because I am currently working full-time in addition to my writing and consulting. Even though it is not my full-time job, I view my writing and consulting as steps toward my long-term goals and ultimate fulfillment.

## Temporary Employment / Internships

The point of an internship is to allow you to work with professionals in a field or line of work in which you are interested, and to develop a network of individuals in that field. Most internships have an end-date, so they are temporary. Because of their temporary nature, you know that if the work is not something that interests you long-term it will eventually come to an end. Internships can turn into permanent jobs.

Look at the big picture while in the internship. Remember that this could lead to future long-term employment. Utilize all areas of communication, including email, within a company to network with people. This is a future employee's opportunity to demonstrate how they could be a strong, full-time hire who is willing to educate themselves on areas in which they have no experience and ask a lot of questions.

The other aspects of temporary employment can involve contract positions or temporary positions that do not have a long-term path but ultimately a simple end date. Even though you know these positions may end, they can help you reach your goals.

The whole point of an internship is to learn, not to make money. It's to develop skills and experience that will make you marketable within a field or a company. Temporary and Contract positions further your development and expand your skills through real experiences, a process that pushes you toward your next opportunity. Temporary and Contract positions both assist in creating yourself as a brand.

Don't give up. One of the most common feelings that a person experiences when doing a job search is the temptation to give up. However, most people don't understand that a job search takes time. You can't turn a switch and suddenly be in a job. You need to be prepared for rejection. Learn from rejection. Rather than taking rejection negatively, find out what you need to do differently or what you may not yet offer that particular company/opportunity. This will give you perspective on how to more accurately market and brand yourself for future jobs.

You need to believe in yourself and your abilities that you bring to a company. Companies sense whether you have confidence in your abilities and skills. The interviewers will ask themselves, "If you are not confident in your abilities and skills, how will you succeed in your job at this company?"

When you are feeling discouraged in your job search, you need to regroup. You can't do a job search when thinking negative thoughts. The easiest way to put your mind in a better place is to remember the goals of your search and reflect on your positive accomplishments in your life. Go as far as writing a list of accomplishments and skills that you have gained over the years. Write down each one and think about how those skills can benefit a company. Use these when marketing yourself to an organization. Make sure to be specific. Don't think of vague examples; consider real examples and skills that can easily demonstrate your ability to affect the company's bottom line.

Here are a few things to keep in mind during a job search: First, a job search can be exhausting and take a lot out of you emotionally and physically. To combat this, practice healthy habits and balance your job search with other things going on in your life. Second, do not allow the job search to cloud your thinking and impair your ability to think clear and perform well. Third, get other people in your life involved in your job search. Communicate your job search challenges to people who care about you. Their advice and support will encourage and nurture you during this challenging time.

Types of Job Searches

There are three main types of job searches: Active, Passive, and Educational. An Active job search is one that has been started because the candidate needs to make a change. That need can be motivated by unemployment, money, career growth, environmental, long-term driven, personal relocation, and many other reasons. It is usually driven by a single goal or reason. It means you are going to make a change no matter what changes in your life from a personal or professional level.

A Passive Job Search is a job search that the candidate has started because of some things about his or her current job that they wish to change, or the current job is not meeting his or her career goals. The passive job search is usually driven by wants rather than needs. Typically passive job searches involve multiple reasons for a possible search but no real end goal. Does that mean you don't have a goal at all? No. The goals of a passive job search is to answer your concerns, determine your feelings, or gauge the mental direction you have in your current job and if you truly need to make changes to better meet those needs. Passive candidates will often times question the point of making a change. They may ask themselves, "Does the job I'm considering really help me or benefit me long term?" Using our goals to reflect on the change will ultimately help answer these questions.

Passive candidates have to constantly remind themselves about what they like or dislike about their current jobs, and how this change will help them achieve their short- or long-term goals. When in doubt, ask yourself the question, "How does this help me step toward my ultimate goal?" Utilize the answer to this question in determining whether the position or job you are considering will be worth the time and energy to pursue. A job search is not recreational; it is a job in itself. Therefore there needs to be a purpose for why you are interviewing for or engaging in conversations about a position.

Another major difference between an Active and Passive candidate is fear – the fear of being unemployed, of not having a job. Many passive candidates do not want to become active because they're afraid of what might happen if they get into an active search. Have you ever heard of the phrase, "The grass is greener on the other side?" You will never know if that is true or not true unless you look to the other side.

Lastly, there are Educational job searches. Most educational job searches involve finding and internship or work that will further your education in a specific field. This, too, has an end goal. Your end goal is to gain experience and education that will ultimately allow you to qualify for the career or employment that you desire for the long-term.

Each of these job searches has to have some type of unique goal or reason for you to be looking. If you don't establish a goal for what you want to accomplish with your search, your search will never be able to satisfy your need or want. Creating this goal is important.

How do you describe your search and where do you see yourself in your search? Active or Educational job seekers typically have thought a lot about their ultimate goals and what they need in order to move forward. They are usually confident and determined in what they want to achieve. Passive job seekers are a little less certain about what they want to do. Often times they are still questioning fulfillment in their career. It does not mean you cannot create goals; just be prepared for those goals to potentially change as you become more active in your search.

Reason for a Job Search

Here are some of the reasons or feelings people typically feel when they are doing a job search, and form a person's goals:

- Unemployment – I was laid off from my previous job and have to get back to work.
- I really enjoy my current job, but I just don't feel like it will provide opportunities that will help me reach my goals.
- My partner or spouse has taken a position in another location and we need to move.
- I cannot afford to pay my bills every month and need to change something in my life to help contribute to my daily living costs.
- Working at my company is great, but the person that I work for does not motivate or lead me in a direction that drives me to be successful.
- I am supposed to be the primary source of income in our relationship, yet my spouse is bringing in more income and, at the same time, feeling overloaded or handling too much.
- I am living in an area that socially has become very dissatisfying to me. I cannot enjoy life where I am living and do not feel that I will be able to accomplish my personal life goals while being in this geographic location.

- My family member is very sick and I have decided that it is important for me to be closer to them.
- I do my job, and I do it well, but I do not feel challenged or fulfilled in what I do on a day-to-day basis.
- I have been an engineer for a while now, and I really want to transition to sales as a career change.
- My company's policies and procedures do not support my own personal beliefs on how a company should work toward treating their employees.
- I cannot afford to live in this area while working in this job.
- I have tried working nights and it is affecting my health. I need to do something about my work schedule so as to project a better and healthier lifestyle for myself and the family around me.
- I want to live closer to my family because of my kids or grandkids.
- In order for me to grow within this company, I have to be able to relocate to different areas of the country long-term, but I do not wish to relocate in the long-term.
- I really want to be in this field, but I do not have any experience that would allow me to enter or prosper in this field at this time.

These are certainly not all the reasons that motivate people to look for a job, but this list gives you a good representation of what people typically think about when doing a job search. These thoughts typically will help generate short-term goals. Think about why you are currently looking. What thoughts do you have? Now use these thoughts to create a short-term goal on why you have decided to look for a position, and commit to these goals. Do not let other people distract you from the goals of your job search. One of the biggest reasons why job changes do not create happiness or success in your long-term goals is because people lose sight of the long-term goals. Is the move you are trying to make a temporary one or a permanent one?

A common mistake that a job seeker makes in her search is that she relies on other people's opinions about a company or an opportunity, which clouds her judgment on the decision to move forward with the opportunity. Just because the company may have bad press does not mean you cannot bring value to the organization. Maybe you can be the person that brings positive change to the company. Just because one person did not like working for a company does not mean you won't like it. Maybe the reason that person did not like working for the company is because the company did not help them get to their goal, but is their goal the same as your goal? It is also important to remember that when a company has negative trends or events that impact the company's long-term goals, this typically leads to positive trends going forward. Wouldn't you want to join the company when they are moving in that positive direction?

Figure out your Ideal Job

In previous chapters we talked about creating your goals to determine what would personally fulfill you in your life's ambitions and ultimate dreams. Now it is time to analyze your different career options to figure out the type of direction you want to go with your career.

There are several steps involved in trying to determine your ideal job situation:

- Look at your current or most recent employment situation. What about that position would you say matched your goals and what would you say did not? Break down the position. The things you liked and the things you did not like. This will help you try to understand whether you need to make significant or minor changes in the direction of your job search.

- Think about your interests and passions and how they are satisfied when you are at work. What things can you bring to your next position that will allow you to be more personally satisfied with your day-to-day work environment?

- Go back and break down your strengths and weakness. Is the job direction you have been in really maximizing your strengths along with finding ways to grow and develop your weaknesses? Is your weakness dragging you down in your ability to grow your career in these types of opportunities?

- Take a look at your technical capabilities that you have obtained in your career. Are you utilizing these and keeping them fresh in your job? Is there a type of job that will help you develop new skills or increase the strengths of your current skills?

- Look at results of your personality assessment and see how it compares to the path that you have chosen. Do your characteristics match that of the type of position you have been in, or are there indications you should likely change your job search in a totally different direction?

- Lastly, how do you define success? Is success based on income, status, or type of responsibilities? Or is success simply feeling rewarded by what you do for others?

Use all the information and things you have taken from these answers to look at the big picture of your job search and what type of job or career path will help you be satisfied while still being able to attain your goals. How far apart or different is your current job from the job that would be ideal for you. Compare the two and come up with a plan on how you are going to change your approach to better align your next steps in your career with your ultimate long-term goals.

There are also long-term goals that you have to strongly consider when making these decisions. What this means is that you do not necessarily have to make all the radical changes in your career or life plan in order to meet your goals. You can continue to take those steps to get to where you want to be. Again, by taking steps toward those career goals in altering how you move in your job one step at a time.

The key to this is positioning you for future job changes and career developments. Obviously you want to actively work on your short-term changes but make sure that they are leading you toward your long-term changes. If your short-term changes lose sight of your long-term goals, then you need to find ways to realign yourself to meet these goals.

## Position's Value to a Company

One additional issue that you need to evaluate when determining the changes you are going to make in your job search and how you are going to approach the position you take, is how you will affect the company's bottom line. Companies are no longer driven on employee loyalty and long-term employee retention as much as changes to an organization to keep a constant revenue stream. What does this mean? If a company decides that using a certain support program that is ran by five internal specialists is no longer saving them the money needed to justify the program, they will cut the program and lay off the specialists. Do they consider they are lying off five loyal employees? No, they are considering how the program affects their bottom line.

A great example of this happened with one of my biggest clients. One day I received a private phone call from a key executive within one of my client companies. He told me that he wanted me to help support any of his people that came to me who were affected by an impending layoff. Many of the people that were going to be affected were good employees, with long-standing years of committed service within the company. I asked him then why they were letting these people go. His response was, "We looked at the organizational chart and determined which positions were effectively costing us more than the ultimate returns and decided to delete those positions across the board." I then asked, "Are you not concerned who the actual people are in the positions?" His response was simple: "This is not about whom they are; this is about the position and how it affects our bottom line and our plan to continue having the profitability that we always planned on."

This is an example of how companies have taken a greater concern on the financial gains of their decision to release an employee, not the loss of the employee themselves. So you have to consider how your skills, experience, and talents that you bring to the table will align with the long-term strategic vision and goals of the impending company in order to bring enough value for you to stay. This is the same with the type of job you choose to be in. What is more important to a company: a person who manages a team of 250 employees, or a support agent that runs a specialized program designed to save the company money, but with no long-term guarantees of doing so? Companies are more inclined to keep someone that has responsibilities over the masses before keeping someone that is a single support agent.

Again, here would be another great example of a great career opportunity that went wrong because of company's lack of value for their employees. A very close friend of mine was the CFO of a company when his boss came to him and offered him a move into a more "strategic" role, where instead of managing people, he would manage lean initiatives within the company. The employment change he was making happening during one of the hardest economic hardships of the company's existence. I warned my friend that taking this position would make him extraordinarily vulnerable for job elimination down the road. Two years later, he got downsized due to an economic restructuring and job elimination. He was with his company for twelve years. He was a very loyal employee, but that did not stop the company from deleting his job.

The key word to remember when looking at your next move is the word value. Every company looks at each employee and tries to determine the true value of that person within the organization. Value can be determined by many facets of a person's role and responsibilities within the company.

Ultimately, how that person affects the bottom line and the profitability of the organization is going to determine what value they bring to the table. Make sure that with any position you consider, look at the true value that you can bring to the organization in that role and how valuable you will be to affecting the bottom-line profitability.

Defining your Target Jobs

It is important to know how to approach your job search and the values of the position you are considering. Look at the big picture and define what role you are looking for in your next position and the value to the company as well as to your career. How do you want to approach your next job and how will it get you to future jobs that will lead to your end long-term goals?

Often candidates make the mistake of relying on the company to dictate what it will take to get them to their long-term goals. You cannot depend on a company's organizational plan to determine how you advance your career. Create a career path in your mind of how you will step up to the long-term goal you are trying to achieve and that will help you define your next target job.

Remember that these roles are not only about in which areas you are most likely to see the greatest gains, but they are also roles in which you are going to see personal and professional satisfaction as well. Use the skills, the personality attributes, and your personal and professional interest when determining a job that will allow you to fundamentally make gains toward your long –term career goals and at the same time feel like you have been successful.

This does not mean you have to narrow your job search to two or three particular fields or jobs. This does not mean that you have to target any particular type of skill. This just means you need to make a fundamental list of jobs and areas that you are willing to consider and explore that you know will help you manage moving forward in your career. It is important, especially in a failing or ailing economy, to keep your job search as broad as possible but still focus it on areas that will benefit you.

Narrowing the Industries and Categories

You need to determine which industries or company categories you want to focus finding a job in. Not every industry is going to react the same as another. Look at the trends of the economy and how each particular industry performed during the changing economic times. Focus on industries and categories that you know will support having someone in a role that you intend to pursue. Put yourself in a positive position where you do not have to worry about your position being cut when times get rough. Also, do not go into an industry that you know is having a hard time staying stable in the harsh economic times.

Combining Elements to Approach your Search

Now that you have your list of target jobs and target industries, you can now take these two areas and combine them together. This is the basis for your job search and will be the force behind how you approach your search. Since it is going to support both aspects that make up a successful career direction in your job search, you will have an easier time driving those successes and steps toward making it to the next goal in your life – leading to that future, long-term goal.

An important thing that you have to take into consideration, when selecting the type of job interest and industries you are going to pursue, is how your lifestyle is going to be affected by these decisions. Knowing that you are going to be happy in the role you choose, are you going to be happy with the lifestyle and environment you are going to live in when choosing a role in this field? Is there a financial shift in how you are going to be able to support yourself, and is the financial shift downward? Even though you are going to be happier in your job, is the downward financial shift going to cause hardship that will decrease your level of happiness?

For people that are unemployed, this can be one of the biggest challenges. You cannot support your lifestyle and survive on unemployment. Often times, people who are unemployed lose complete sight of where they are headed in the long-term just because they become distracted by the process of getting into a position. The most important thing to remember is that the job you take may not be propelling you toward your goals, but might be a small step in the right direction.

You always have to remember the big picture when looking at each of the several steps in finding your next job. Take into consideration each move and how it will impact your life and your life's direction. Do not make sacrifices when choices can be made that will allow you to avoid those sacrifices. But, if you choose or are forced to sacrifice, the most important thing is make sure you are going to be happy with that decision. It is very important to remain focused on your long-term career goals and ultimate career fulfillment and satisfaction. Personal sacrifices are oftentimes found to be acceptable when it means fulfilling and satisfying your career goals.

Remember that when defining your job search you have to remember all the major elements in the job search that will drive you long-term. Keep all aspects of your decision in mind and consider how they will affect you overall. Do not forget each variable that you have defined as important so that you do not feel like you have lost more than you have gained.

In the broad scheme of things, a job search is never a hard science. There is not a right or wrong way to handle your search as long as you are fulfilling all the commitments that you made to yourself. Make sure you stick by your commitments. Review the lists you have made, think about the plans you defined, remember the goals you set, and make the job search decisions that will be personally fulfilling for you in the long-term.

Tim needs to get back into a full-time position. He is actively searching for the right opportunity to continue his career in the manufacturing industry. Because he was fulfilled in his last role, he decides that getting with an organization in a Manufacturing Manager, Lean Change Agent, or even a Corporate Manufacturing capacity would continue his fulfillment and help him market his skills. He has a very strong background in Lean Operations and Six Sigma, and knows how valuable these skills can be. Although he would love to work for a larger company, he realizes that smaller, privately-held companies may be more apt to respect his experience regardless of his lack of a degree.

Samantha is not fulfilled in her current job, but she is content. She is passively looking because she really wants to see if she can find true fulfillment in a job change. She already knows she wants to get into a more brand management type of position. She has skills from her business in generating private label brand development of energy service options for the community and corporate world. Although not 100% transferable to consumer products, she realizes that the best direction for her to specialize in brand management is to switch industries. She has tremendous skills and experience in developing brand strategies within the energy industry, and all her personality tests show that she has the personality traits to drive a business unit. Her goal is to land a brand management position with a medium to large Consumer Products Company even if it means potentially getting in entry-level.

George has been unemployed for way too long and is actively looking to get back in to a full-time position. He clearly has decided to try to apply his finance abilities in different areas. While in his past positions he has been a financial and investment manager for personal and private investment accounts, he now feels he can take this to a different direction and be an investment manager in the corporate world. The industry really doesn't matter, but he knows that companies are looking for people to build their values through the back end investments of their assets. His goal is to get with a small to medium size company that is looking to use its assets and position itself to grow in this tough economy through smart investing.

Pete is graduating college and knows the market is tough. He is taking two approaches: he is looking at full-time positions and internships. He had a very good friend that took a "corporate internship" out of college with the promise that it would turn into a full-time opportunity. So he is not ruling out the option. He wants to get into the service or manufacturing industry where he can coach and mentor people. All the personality tests and evaluations he has had in his college major have identified him as a future leader and manager. Pete is going to focus on getting into an entry-level management trainee position within a company where he knows he can further develop his leadership skills.

# BUILDING A RESUME/COVER LETTER

One of the biggest challenges for most candidates is building a résumé. A resume is not just thrown together, but needs to be built and developed over the course of time. You need to put a lot of care in to building the foundation of your resume and then creating the value you that will sell your resume to a company. There are countless articles and books on the topic that contradict each other on the dos and don'ts of writing a résumé. Rather than giving you "the way it needs to be," let's look at the advantages and disadvantages of each part of the résumé and how you style it, write it, and present it.

Think of your résumé as the first tool in getting interest from a future employer. What do you want the person on the other end to see on your résumé? What is the goal that you want your résumé to accomplish when the hiring authority reads it?

Here are some questions to consider:

- Does your résumé indicate the direction you have taken your career and where you want your career to continue to lead?
- Have you established a clear goal or reason on why you are submitting your résumé?
- When a person looks at your résumé, does it clearly define your work experience in the areas of your specialty? (There are definitely limitations on how many years you want to reflect on your résumé. This will be discussed later in this chapter.)
- Is your résumé communicating not only the experience that you have gained, but how you have further educated yourself during your career?
- Does the résumé define your responsibilities at recent jobs and the objectives or purposes the job met for the company?

- Does your résumé highlight accomplishments and ways you have impacted the bottom lines of the organizations you have worked for?
- What monetary or measurable ways have you impacted your previous employer's bottom lines?
- Have you offered the potential employer enough information to interest them in learning how you will provide value to their company?
- Does the résumé allow your interviewers to understand your technical knowledge in the field that you have been involved in?
- Do the job titles on your résumé clearly reflect the significance of your role and do they clearly depict the responsibilities you held with the organization?
- Have you presented all available assets, skills, experiences, and education that would affect your ability to be valuable to this future employer?

As you can see, a résumé can provide an abundance of information to a potential employer and can allow that person to evaluate your ability to perform the functions of the job. This is also a critical stage of the job search process because most of the time the résumé is your way to create a discussion between yourself and the company or on the job that you are pursuing. So, while you may think your résumé speaks for itself, go back and review the above questions to make sure your résumé answers them.

Chronological vs. Functional (or even Combination)
When building a résumé, you must determine the most effective format, which brings us to the ever-so-popular debate of Chronological versus Functional résumés. These are the two main ways to format a résumé. However, a trend that is becoming increasingly common is bringing the advantages of both styles into one résumé. It is easiest to define a résumé

on how you present your work experience, skills, and accomplishments. The simplest way to define the difference between the two is that a Chronological résumé shows a clear and defined work history and where you gained your experiences and accomplishments within your work history. It presents your work history in chronological order, starting with the most recent job in your career, and moves backwards to show where you gained your knowledge and experiences. A Functional résumé shows the experiences, accomplishments, and skills you bring to the table and places less emphasis on the actual companies or places you have worked and the positions you have held. This type of résumé typically places the work history, along with dates of employment, toward the bottom of the résumé.

Although there are strengths to both of these résumé approaches, I have a clear opinion on what I believe is the stronger approach, but you have to ask yourself what are you trying to achieve by presenting your résumé in front of a company. Do you want the company to focus on where you worked and the positions you have held, or do you want them to focus on what you have gained or accomplished? Or do you want both?

Chronological résumés have advantages and disadvantages to them. The following are some of the important advantages of Chronological résumés:

- Clearly defines the path you have taken in your career, when you attained certain knowledge, accomplished tasks and goals in your life, and where you are in your career.
- Easily presents where you started in your career and suggests a trajectory. Where are you at today? Often times the hiring authority will ask themselves how the position being offered would help the candidate continue to progress toward their long-term goals as evidenced by the résumé.
- The hiring authority does not have to figure out where you gained your knowledge, or what your position or responsibilities

were when you achieved your accomplishments. There seldom is a doubt on how you acquired the skills and experiences for which you have been awarded, or what you might lack in experience or knowledge.

- Résumés that are written in a chronological order typically present themselves as being more factual than persuasive. Job-seekers who use this type of résumé believe that their skills, experience, and education sell themselves.
- Chronological format is the most common and most widely accepted form of résumé in job searching.

Some of the disadvantages of Chronological résumés include the following:

- If the goal of job-seekers is to change the directions of their careers, this résumé style can impede their ability to convince a hiring authority of their commitment to that career change.
- This type of résumé clearly shows a career path factually defined and clearly laid out. This allows the hiring authority to pass judgment on the logic behind your changes and moving into this role. The hiring authority can clearly be subjective on whether the job you are applying for will meet your goals without asking you what your goals are.
- Résumés that are chronological, because they are so factual, can oftentimes highlight areas of weakness, lack of knowledge or skills, and inability to gain achievements in the positions you have held. It makes it easier for hiring authorities to see speed bumps and hurdles you have had in your career without allowing the opportunity to explain them.
- If there are gaps in your résumé, or periods where you have left the industry or changed fields, there is no ethical way of keeping the hiring authority from seeing this. That leaves questions in

the hiring authority's mind that you will have to address at some point in the interview process.

- Since the résumé has explanations of when you achieved or experienced certain types of experiences in your career, the hiring authority can also determine whether they feel your experience is outdated.
- Ageism – None of us want to admit that employers can be ageist. Unfortunately, it happens even though it is not legal. How you present a chronological résumé and how much of your experience you present clearly offers an employer an opportunity to pass judgment based on age and years in the business.

Functional Résumés have advantages and disadvantages to them.  The following is a list of some of the important advantages of Functional Résumés:

- If you are attempting to change directions in your career or pursue a different field or industry, these types of résumés can be advantageous because you're focusing the hiring authority on your experience and skills and not on the jobs and work history you have experienced.
- If your career has been plagued with frequent changes in jobs and companies due to reasons beyond your control, a functional résumé can help detract from your job changes and focus the company on the skills you acquired.
- For people with limited experience or even coming directly out of college, these types of résumés will help reflect how the skills they have acquired over the years through other avenues can benefit the company.

- In the event you find yourself looking to take steps backward in your career, using this résumé will help prevent a hiring authority from thinking that you are overqualified for a position.
- If you have gaps in your employment, whether purposeful or not, the functional résumé format, again, takes the focus away from those gaps and centers them on your background.

Some of the disadvantages of Functional Résumés:
- Companies do not see a clear picture of your career path, past growth and abilities to grow, or level of experience based on your time with companies.
- Hiring authorities have to figure out where you actually gained experience. This makes it difficult for them to determine if your skills are current or dated, which may factor into whether you get the job.
- Hiring authorities could think that the reason you are presenting a functional résumé is because you are trying to overshadow negative occurrences in your work history. Companies will think you are creating a diversion from the truth of your background and changing their focal point. Basically, it could make the hiring authority question your credibility and integrity.

Combination resumes are resumes that combine many of the strengths of a chronological resume with some of the values of a functional resume. Ultimately the best thing about a functional resume is the added accomplishments and successes you often times find highlighted on a functional resume.

## Breaking down a Résumé

By reviewing a sample résumé and making sense of its different parts, you will better understand how you should present your background. To make the explanation clearer and easier to understand, we are going to focus on a Chronological Résumé since it is the most widely used résumé in job searches.

Remember what goals you are trying to achieve with your résumé. The ultimate purpose for a résumé is to market the skills, experience, education, and background that would be help future employers to see the value in you as a candidate. Regardless of your goals presented by your résumé, the résumé will help you attain success in achieving this goal.

## Formatting Basics

There are ways to utilize your formatting to help not only present your experience with clarity and concision, but to also utilize the most space on the paper. One of the biggest mistakes people make is leaving "dead space" or "white space" on the paper. Empty, wasted space makes your résumé longer and limits how much information it can present.

The following are ways to minimize this type of space problem:

- Putting as much information on a single line. Common mistakes are using three lines to write out your contact information (address, number, e-mail, etc.) where it is just as easy to put it on one line separating each by a bullet or hyphen.

Examples presented below:

Good use of space

124 Smithfield Ln.- Anywhere, US 12345 – (123) 456-7890 – bc@mail.com

Poor use of space

124 Smithfield Ln

Anywhere, US 12345

(123) 456-7890

bc@mail.com

- Looking for dangling words referred to as "hangers." These are lines on a page that only have two or three words before the end of a bullet or a sentence. Find a way to delete or edit the sentence to cut down those three words and bring the line up to the line above.

Examples presented below:

Good use of space

Lead a team of 20-30 employees in an office environment on administrative and support.

Poor use of space

Lead a team of 20 or 30 hourly employees in an office environment on administrative and support tasks including, accounting and janitorial.

- Avoid extra spaces between sections or areas of your résumé. It is not necessary to put more than one extra space between each section for the hiring authority to understand and read it well.
- It is easier for a person to understand, read, and absorb a person's background when it is formatted in a bullet point format versus a paragraph format. This also allows the job-seeker to avoid the use of "I" and increase the use of action words.

Examples presented below:

<u>Good use of formatting</u>

- Lead a team of 20 or 30 hourly employees in an office environment on administrative and support tasks.
- Managed the departmental budget and P&L ensuring compliance and accomplish the company's profitability goals.

<u>Poor use of formatting</u>

During my time in this role I lead a team of 20 or 30 hourly employees in an office environment on administrative and support tasks. I was also responsible for managing the departmental budget and P&L, ensuring compliance, and accomplishing the company's profitability goals.

- Be aware of the length of your résumé. Here are some simple rules to go by. First, lose the misconception that every person has to have a one-page résumé. This is a huge myth in the industry. If you are presenting a résumé where you lack a tremendous amount of experience in the industry, you are looking for a career change, or you are entry-level or a new high school/college graduate, you should limit your résumé to one page. If you have more than 3-5 years of experience in any particular profession or industry, it is acceptable to have up to a two-page résumé. For those candidates who are in industries where positions often require extended education such as Ph.D. or J.D., exceeding two pages is typically accepted. Often these people have been published or written articles or books, or are in an industry that has the need for an extensive amount of specialized skills, training, and program knowledge, which justify a longer résumé.
- Do not repeat bullets merely because you have been in similar roles throughout your career. Take the time to make unique

bullets for each of your positions. Although you may have functioned in the same or in similar roles multiple times, you want the hiring authority to feel you continued to grow and gain additional knowledge and experience. Some time ago, a candidate sent me his résumé with the same bullets for each of his jobs. I asked him why he did this, and he said it was because nothing ever changed. I suggested not using the résumé as it was, but he insisted this is how he wanted to move forward. When we sent his résumé to the company, their immediate response was they were not interested because the candidate did not take the time to write a résumé that shows he values his career move and put forth effort when writing his résumé. Cutting corners on the résumé is definitely not effective.

- Never use italics! It has been studied by many eye-motion specialists that using italics makes a résumé difficult to read and comprehend. Take advantage of bolding, underlining, and indenting as well as the alignment of paragraphs or lines. You want to use bolding and underlining typically to highlight who you worked for, positions you have held, and specific education, skills, and experiences that you know will be extraordinarily valuable in gaining your next position.

- Stop using fancy or animated fonts. Presenting a résumé with a script font does not make the résumé seem more "personal" to the reader; it just makes it harder to read. Stick to functional and easy-to-read fonts like Arial and Times New Roman, which are the most commonly used fonts when writing resumes.

- When presenting your application via email or internet, do not put a cover letter and a résumé in the same document. Your résumé (also referred to as a Curriculum Vitae or CV for short), should be the only thing that a person sees when opening up the document. Cover letters can be presented in a separate document or attachment.

- Make sure to utilize the dynamics of the language that you speak to present your credentials. Use a thesaurus to find synonyms to describe your experiences or skills. You do not want to use the same verb repetitively.

- When writing bullets, do not just put two or three words on a line. Although it does not need to be a complete sentence, the sentence fragment should clearly represent the thoughts you are trying to communicate to the hiring authority and you need to fill white space.

Résumé Sections

There are many possible sections to a résumé. This is not going to be an exhaustive list of sections you can have on your résumé. However, this will address many potential issues that people present when writing and presenting a résumé.

- Objective: Every résumé does not have to have an objective. Many people think it is mandatory. The only point to an objective or cover letter is to help the hiring authority understand why you are applying for the job and where you want to go in your career. Make sure in the Objective section you clearly tell them what you are trying to pursue and avoid talking subjectively about yourself. If you need to emphasize the change in your career and new goals that are not clear on your résumé, I would recommend an objective over a cover letter because cover letters are not often looked at by hiring managers. However, if your résumé clearly defines your career objective and goals, you do not need to utilize either (cover letter or objective). I tend to side against both unless absolutely necessary.

- Summary of Qualifications: This is an excellent way to present a highlight of your qualifications. You want the hiring authority to have an interest to learn more about your background. By presenting valuable skills, experiences, and accomplishments that would relate to the position you are applying for, you are giving them a reason to continue reviewing your credentials. Often times this can be done in a table format with short, two- or three-word bullets, or in a bullet point format similar to what you will use to create your employment history. Also, you should consider customizing this for the skills needed for the position you are applying for.

Example of this:

- 3+ Years Auditing Experience
- Financial Reporting/Variances
- Cost Basis
- Microsoft Office

- WMS/Inventory Systems
- Inventory Analysis
- Project Management
- Bilingual Spanish/English

- Education: If you have educational accomplishments that are deemed valuable in your industry, you want to make sure this is at the beginning of your résumé rather than at the end. I cannot tell you how many times I have picked up a résumé for a job that requires a degree and the person has it hidden toward the back or bottom of the résumé. Make sure it is highlighted at the top, especially if the position requires it. If you do not have the educational requirements for the job, then move your educational information toward the end of the résumé in order to allow the hiring authority to view your credentials first. Another major problem in today's employment market is unaccredited online schools. Many candidates that have not acquired a two- or four-year degree get solicited by online unaccredited programs with the promise that they can get a degree through an accelerated process without having to do a lot of the work at a brick-and-mortar school with an accredited program. These online degree programs are known as "degree mills." These companies basically sell you a piece of paper. Most of these colleges will ask you for thousands of dollars and promise you a degree in six months or fewer. Sometimes these degrees are referred to as "life experience" degrees awarded against the work experience you have acquired. These are not accredited degree programs. Make sure that if you are approached by or look into an online degree program that they meet the requirements of accreditation with the US Department of Education. You can go on the government's website to learn more about the accrediting bodies that make a college an actual accredited college. Stating that your education is "equivalent to a US Bachelor's Degree" is only valid if it is evaluated and accredited by a US Accredited College/University. If you have obtained an unaccredited degree, you are better off not listing it on your résumé. If you list it on your résumé and do not clearly make the company aware that it was an online program that was unaccredited, the company may feel you were manipulating the truth and decide not to hire you, or even worse, rescind the offer they have already made to you. Also, just because the country you are from states your education is "Bachelor Level," you also should have it evaluated and accredited here in the United States by an accredited college or university.

- Employment History: Make sure to clearly highlight the company you worked for, the position you held, and the timetable you were in each position. I often see résumés where candidates list being at a company for seven years and holding four positions but do not specifying how long or when they were in each position. If you worked for a company for a number of years and held different positions and titles, make sure to explain the different positions and clearly show how they differ and the timetable you were in each role. No one starts their career as a Vice President or COO (unless you owned your own business). So make sure you put the position you started in and show the natural progression. For each of your past positions, make sure you not only discuss objectives and responsibilities of the position, but also the accomplishments you had in those roles. You do not want the hiring authority to have to assume what experiences you have had; what they assume may not be an accurate reflection of your experience. I will discuss this later in this chapter.

- Technical Skills: In this section, you can highlight various technical skills and knowledge you have acquired over the years that may be beneficial to the hiring authority. Divide these skills into bullets that target each type of technical skill. For example, group all computer skills together into one bullet and fill up the line from left to right.

- Other Education and Training: You can talk about how you have acquired further education and training in your field to help you become better at your job. This demonstrates to a hiring authority that you have an interest in growing personally, not only professionally.

- References: Do not list references on your résumé unless your work experience is limited. It is unnecessary to give this information at the onset of discussions. At some point during the conversations with the hiring authority, they will ask for references if it is important for the process. Simply indicate that "references are available upon request."

<u>Use of Bullets</u>

What you say and how you present bullets tells the hiring authority quite a lot about you. One of the most significant things to remember when writing bullets is to create value to the company. If what you are writing is not going to be valuable, then don't write it. Minimize the use of "I" or "me," and utilize the words that are more team-based or action specific.

The first person point of view (using "I," "we," and "me") is implied by a résumé, especially when you format it in bullet point form. This gives you an opportunity to use action words to emphasize your ability to drive change and create an impact within an organization. Do not just use action words that are singular directed but also use those words that create a sense of collaboration or working with teams. Example of this would be "lead vs. partnered" or "mediated vs. collaborated."

Here are some examples of commonly used and effective action words:
- Adapted
- Analyzed
- Coached
- Collaborated
- Contributed
- Coordinated
- Designed
- Developed
- Diagnosed
- Evaluated
- Forecasted
- Guided
- Increased
- Instructed
- Managed
- Mediated

- Motivated
- Participated
- Persuaded
- Reduced

When you are writing bullets that describe your general objective of your job and responsibilities, make sure to be specific. If you managed people, how many people did you manage? If you oversaw the budget, how much money were you responsible for? If you oversaw volume, what was the volume? The use of numbers is the area that people most lack on a résumé. Statistics of your past capabilities and performance enable a company to get a measurable picture of your capabilities and performance.

When writing bullets that are highlighting accomplishments, make sure you create a clear picture of what you accomplished. Another easy way to explain this is similar to "situation, action, and result" style interviewing. This will be discussed in greater length in an upcoming chapter. But the basics of this are to describe a situation, to discuss how you engaged the problem, and to synthesize the end results.

Make sure to employ numbers to show how your actions changed the bottom line to make money for the company.

Example of this:
- Identified high variances in raw materials and product consumption for finished goods. Implemented a bar-code scanning system to better track raw materials and usage, which decreased variances from 12% to 3%.

Examples of types of things you can talk about within your bullets:
- How many people did you manage?
- What was the volume (i.e. number of transactions, number of orders, and number of calls)?

- How large was the budget, P&L, or sales you were responsible for?
- How many items did you process per hour, per week, per year?
- What was your success rate?
- Financial or percentage value of your yields?

Cover Letters

I am definitely not a huge supporter of cover letters. The biggest reason why is because people have a tendency to make cover letters subjective opinions about themselves and not factual. When someone uses a cover letter, there is a risk that it, along with the résumé, might be thrown away because often times the reader doesn't see the value in a cover letter. Many hiring authorities simply throw the letter away and look directly at the resume. Often times it is used when the résumé or objective does not directly reflect the job-seeker's purpose of applying or true abilities to do the job he or she is applying for. Your cover letter will be scanned for a few moments; make it clear and concise. Limit yourself to the most important facts and get directly to the point of the cover letter. Make sure you address your cover letter to the person you intend to read it. You can use your cover letter to highlight many things including goals of your career, beneficial experience that may not be easily seen on your résumé, and a snapshot of your educational or other training. Cover letters are not a pre-interview. Do not try to "sell" yourself through a cover letter; simply bring to the surface things that may not be seen on your résumé. It is very important, however, to remember that most cover letters are discarded without even being read. So try to utilize your résumé in reflecting important information and avoid using a cover letter if possible.

A résumé may be concerning to the company. Companies will notice frequent job changes without career advancement, gaps in employment history, years of experience or lack of experience, and will pay attention to salary history and requirements. You obviously cannot lie on your résumé or change what is fact, but certain things should definitely be on a résumé and certain things should not. It definitely is not appropriate to list salary history on a résumé because this encourages the company to assume your needs without discussing them with you. You can choose how much or little experience you put on your résumé based on the needs of the company. When you put thirty years of experience on your résumé, hiring authorities, in the back of their minds, will "date" you and will start questioning your long-term motivations to continue working. They will likely ask themselves, "When does this person plan to retire?" or "How long do they plan on working?"

The challenge is that you do not want there to be years for which your résumé does not account. If your résumé starts with you as a Director (starting 25 years ago) then it is pretty clear you are leaving something off. The hiring authorities will wonder what you had been doing for the prior 25 years. Make sure you develop a good flow and demonstration of your career progression but do not feel you have to include your entire work history, especially if it is not going to bring much added value. Use your own best judgment on what you think is going to help you and what you think is going to hurt you. The key is to make sure that when a person picks up your résumé it seems like you started your career at a certain level and progressed naturally upward throughout your career.

With job changes and gaps, it is best to briefly explain them on the résumé or in a cover letter rather than to leave it vague, allowing the company to question your employment stability. Often a short explanation in parenthesis, such as, "(business closed)," will prevent a company from passing judgment and encourage them to look beyond the gap or short tenure.

Another thing to remember is that companies take seconds, not minutes, to look for keywords on a résumé that make the résumé stand out. Make sure that you use the keywords on your résumé that companies look for in the industry. Remember that not every company carries the same job titles and verbiage when talking about different positions. In my industry, there are dozens of ways to say Production Supervisor. It is important that if you have a job title, verbiage that describes the position, or anything that is distinct from the rest of the industry, you need to go into more detail or clarification. Help the reader understand what you have done and who you are.

Finally, when writing a résumé and cover letter, do not be subjective. People do not want to know what you think of yourself. No one is likely to put on their résumé, "I am a bad communicator;" they will nearly always claim they have excellent communication skills. The information you present to an employer should be factual and create value to them on why you would be a good addition to their organization. It should not be your subjective opinion of yourself.

Here are some basic tips you should remember while revising your cover letter and résumé:

- Check for spelling and grammar mistakes! One of the worst and most common mistakes is presenting/sending a résumé or cover letter with mistakes. Ask multiple people to look at your résumé to make sure this is avoided. Another way to avoid spelling errors is to read your résumé word-for-word backwards. This prevents your brain from perceiving the correct spelling even though the word is spelled wrong. The most frequently misspelled word on a résumé is manager (spelled manger with one 'a' instead of two). Spell-check doesn't catch this error because manger is a legitimate word.
- Avoid subjective phrases and comments such as "strong leader" or "excellent communication skills."
- Make sure that your résumé and cover letter clearly presents the goal of your search and what you are looking to do for the company.

- Use action-, leadership-, and team-based terminology. Make sure a company feels how you are going to impact their organization, not just sees it. Give values to how you have affected the company given specific values on how you affected the bottom line. ("increased efficiencies by 17%, decreased turnover by 3%, reduced loss time accidents from 3 to 1 in the last fiscal year)

- Put the most important factual information at the top of your résumé. Make sure to put information toward the front that will create an initial interest to the hiring authority and a desire to finish reading your paperwork.

- Make sure when listing equipment experience, technical skills, and other "lists" that you use the entire line rather than break them down into separate bullets, which is a poor use of space on your résumé. The order in which you introduce categories on your résumé will depend on your industry. In the IT world, technical knowledge is extremely important and generally should be toward the top – In the Sales world, technical knowledge is secondary and often times can be placed toward the end.

- Do not be too personal. This is true in all interviewing and job-searching situations. Do not use slang words or phrases that are impersonal, such as "yeah," "gotcha," "no kidding," "you know," etc.

- Unless you are applying for a job where your looks are important, do NOT put a picture on your résumé. For instance, a résumé for sales and marketing positions should NOT include a headshot. There are very few careers for which a personal photo would be appropriate. By putting your picture on your résumé, you are encouraging the company to make a decision based on your looks, ethnicity, age, sex, etc.

- Do not fabricate information on your résumé to eliminate gaps or concerns. This is especially important when a reader sees no gaps in the month and year you were in each job. One way to minimize gaps is to utilize years only avoiding placing the month and the year you were in a position. However it is important not to change the years you worked at a company because it will likely be verified before hire. Most companies perform background checks, which include employment and education verification. It is easier to explain a gap than to justify why you lied.
- Do not omit dates of employment. When you do this, you are drawing attention to the potential gaps in your work history or your years of experience.
- Do not put personal information, including hobbies, on your résumé unless it has a direct correlation with the job. Especially avoid talking about your family, marital status, physical characteristics, and number of kids or age of family members.
- Avoid using résumé templates offered by many word processing programs. Try to make your résumé unique to you.
- Do not use fancy lettering, script fonts, designs, graphics, or pictures unless the position specifically is driven on your ability to do so. The most common fonts used on a résumé are "Times New Roman" or "Arial" depending on whether you want to use a san serif or serif font. Do not use fonts that appear to be cursive or "handwriting style" since it can be hard to read and overly casual.
- Never make your typeface is no smaller than 9 pts and never larger than 12 pts. Ideally a résumé should be in 10 pt font.
- To avoid age discrimination, leave off years you graduated college, especially if it was over 20 years, and do not list experience beyond 25 years. When you indicate you have 35

years of experience you are telling the interviewer that you are at least in your early 50s, depending on whether you have a degree.

- Make sure that the e-mail that you list on your résumé is professional. Listing e-mails such as ladykiller72@aol.com or ready2retire@aol.com will not help you to obtain a new position.

Now that you have put together a package with which you can market yourself to a company, you now have to find a way to establish yourself as a brand that represents what a company needs.

Tim wants to detract people from the fact that he doesn't have a degree. He does have further education at the college level but never completed it. He moves the education section to the bottom of his resume. He lists the college he attended and the major he studied in, he just doesn't identify having a degree. He then puts a focus on highlighting his Six Sigma and Lean experience in his Summary of Qualifications and then under each job puts at least 5-7 bullets highlighting how he has increased efficiencies, decreased waste, and made companies more profitable. He uses a lot of numerical examples on how he has impacted the bottom line to show true value in his experience.

Samantha needs to highlight all her branding capabilities. So at the top of her resume she expands the Summary of Qualifications by not only have a block of bullets talking about her branding capabilities, but lists a bunch of bullets on programs and strategies she has implemented and designed selling branded energy services through private companies. She also adds an often avoided objective at the top explaining that she wants to get in a more brand management capacity.

George realizes that many think he is ready for retirement. He changes his email from ready2retire@aol.com to georgebw@aol.com to get people away from the fact that he is older. He takes the dates off his education/certifications and cuts his work history off at 25 years when he was an account manager for a leading consumer financial services company. By doing all this he positions his resume to show that he has some life left in his career.

Pete is a college kid with some, but little experience. He uses the bullets at the top Summary of Qualifications section to truly create pop in his background. He highlights his Training, Leadership, Coaching, Management, and Business Development background that he truly has in managing in a bar. He also highlights all the coursework that relates to business under his education. At the bottom he makes sure to note all the software and technical knowledge and capabilities he has. He knows doing all this will help really beef up his resume and show potential employers that he has a lot to offer.

# BRANDING YOURSELF

When looking at a job search, you have to consider what you are trying to accomplish. Ultimately, you are trying to get a company to recognize its need for your skills, experience, and expertise. In other words, you must market yourself to the company so they perceive you as a product they need. This is called branding.

Branding yourself means to create an image of a key benefit that you bring to the consumer. In this case, you are creating an image of what you can do to benefit the company's short- and long-term goals and vision. Creating yourself into a brand is achieved similarly to creating a product brand. A product is a type of consumable or item that we seek to purchase, where as a brand is an actual name brand or company brand identified within that product group. For example the product – bread sold in stores can be many different brands - Arnold, Pepperidge Farms, or Wonder Bread.

The concept of branding is when we start referring to product in a category as an actual brand we commonly associate with rather than the product itself. When you walk into a restaurant and ask for a soda, do you ask for a soda or do you ask for a Coke? Coke is a brand of a product type (soda) that is commonly requested by a brand not by the type of product. Hence, when you go in to a restaurant often times you ask for a "Coke" rather than a soda. Or when you have a headache, do you ask for an aspirin? Most people will ask for Tylenol. Or when you have to blow your nose, do you ask for a tissue? Most people ask for a Kleenex. Consumers often times ask for these brands because they have been conditioned to think of them as a type of product not an actual brand.

So how does this have anything to do with branding yourself? When a company, manager, or hiring authority needs to solve a problem, you want them to think of you as the solution. This is product branding. Products bring solutions to people's needs or problems.

Branding yourself is important when you are trying to sell yourself to a particular employer or company. While creating a brand, you are creating a solution-based thought of how you will benefit them. Think of it as buying a cleaning product. They all claim they can clean the surface, but what makes one particular product stand out more than others? How do you, as a brand, stand out more than anyone else with similar skills and experience?

You need to look at branding yourself to a company as forming a partnership with the company. Sure, you are providing a solution, but you also want that solution to be ongoing. Helping the company accelerate its success through a partnership that also helps you grow means you are creating a better and more recognizable brand in yourself.

Knowing your Target Audience

The first thing you need to think about when creating a brand for yourself is to remember who your target audience is and the ultimate goal of your job search. What type of company are you targeting? What skill set or profession are you targeting to work in? Are you going to work in a blue collar or a white collar environment? Branding yourself for a manufacturing plant is completely different than branding you for a corporate finance department.

Once you have determined the focal point and recipient you intend to present your resume to, you need to package your "product" for that audience. This includes writing your resume, performing your search and whom you target, considering how to approach the phone interview and the in-person interview, following up, and ultimately presenting your skills and experience.

Research the Companies and the Industry

Start by doing research and asking questions of potential employers on what their needs are in a person with your experience. You need to ask questions to truly know how to present yourself. Do not be afraid to ask potential employers what their expectations and needs of the person they plan to hire. If they need someone that can work with a certain program and you have experience working with a similar program of a competitor, you have to find a way to sell not just that skill, but other skills to counter balance what you are lacking. Find out what skills and experiences are of benefit to potential employers.

Research the current needs and trends within your industry or job category. Find out terminology, phrases, methodologies, and skills that are valued and make sure you present those that you have experience in clearly to the people you are marketing to. If a company needs someone who can balance a P&L and you have done this in your last three positions, this is something to market to the company. However, if the position is not responsible for the P&L then marketing this skill would have no relevance and not help position you well for the role. Know what the employer is seeking before marketing the different skills you possess.

Targeting the needs of Companies/Industries

Now that you have determined the typical needs of your target companies and hiring authorities, and have researched the trends of the industry, now you have to find ways that you will benefit the needs of that end target. Utilize this knowledge to incorporate these things in all aspects of the interview and marketing process. This includes highlighting these items on your resume, in the phone screening, during the interview, and post-interview follow-up.

Do not forget that not only do you need to look at specific skills and experiences you have gained and acquired over the years, but often times you need to look at the personality, style, and image that a company is trying to portray with the people that they hire. For instance, you will find it very rare that a male salesperson would be selling women's beauty aid products. Or an engineer whose job it is to design handicapped adapted vehicles having never been around a person that is in a wheelchair. You have to make sure what you are marketing to you target audience that makes sense.

## Turning Weaknesses into Strengths

Anytime you have a weakness or a flaw that you know is going to detract a hiring authority's interest, you need to counter balance this with your strengths. This does not mean that you will get them to look past your weakness, but by highlighting strengths that make you an attractive candidate encourages the hiring authority to feel more comfortable hiring you regardless of your weaknesses.

## Determine the Demands

Determine what demands for skills exist within your industry and the companies in your search. Use this knowledge to leverage your strengths against your weaknesses. This again involves understanding the market and the industry you are in.

Another important factor to remember is that 80-85% of jobs that companies actually fill are typically not posted or advertised. This means that the company or hiring manager you are approaching may not necessarily be looking at you for a position that they appear to have open. So don't limit how you market or brand yourself to what you think they specifically have a need for today.

You need to think more broadly about your marketing approach. Learn about the company. For instance, a very good client of mine focuses a significant portion of their strategies on environmental initiatives. So when marketing to this company, even if you are marketing yourself as an administrative person, you can highlight anything you have done that has helped the environment or supports that corporation's vision.

Remember that throughout the hiring and engagement process; always ask questions to learn more about the organizational needs of the company and the direction they have been pursuing. You could never have too much information. If you cannot ask any questions then you probably are not interested enough in working for the company. Even after 12 years of being with my most recent employer, I learn new things about the company every day.

## The Point of Branding Yourself

Branding yourself is more than being a hard worker and placing hope in the idea that the company or manager will see reason to hire or promote you. Branding yourself is constantly promoting ongoing benefits to the person(s) on how you will continue to help the company grow while you continue to growing yourself.

You need to understand the strengths you have acquired over the years and present them to the hiring authority such that it becomes obvious to them that you will use your strengths to build their organization, and that you are also willing to work on turning your weaknesses into strengths in order to help grow yourself along with the company.

## Creating Value in your Community Involvements

Get involved in as many organizations, team exercises, professional groups, online forums, and educational events. You need to create an image for yourself. People need to know that you have something more to offer than the guy sitting next to you. As you get more involved and engaged in more things, you will find that you provide a broader scope of benefits to that ever-evolving consumer (in many cases a company or future employer).

For you to get involved in programs and organizations means networking and using the technologies that have been provided to us over the years. This means you need to familiarize yourself with new technologies and finding ways for them to help you market yourself more effectively.  Do a personal assessment of how you are utilizing today's programs, systems, and technologies. If you notice deficiencies in this area, find further training to get yourself to a level where you can maximize the resources available to you.

## Approaching Changes in Companies

Evaluate techniques you utilize in approaching changes in a company and how you implement and respond to change. What would you do first if you walk into a department that is in shambles and you are not the department manager? How do you approach making the department not only better for you to work in, but better for that manager and the company? What types of strategies and approaches would you use? How might you present this perspective to your hiring authority? Be prepared to describe how you would handle the situations you have experienced or how you would handle fictitious scenarios. It is important to go into detail because companies are trying to evaluate how well your practices would work within their environment.

## Evolving Process of Branding

There are several reasons why branding yourself is an ongoing process. First and foremost, companies are always evolving. If you think even a company's mission or vision always stays the same then you really need to take a business management class. A company constantly evolves, and it's because of this that you should be evolving your brand to the company's needs. Branding yourself should occur while working in your current position as well as when in a job search. The other factor that drives the constant changing of your brand is the changing of the people. As new people become part of your everyday work environment, especially when these new people are important people within an organization, the initiatives, needs, and direction of the company may change. Be prepared to evolve your brand to accommodate such a changing environment.

## Creating an Attitude

Attitude plays a key role in your efforts to market yourself. Confident people demonstrate confidence in the interview process; hence they will typically get selected before someone that lacks confidence. This starts from the second you wake-up in the morning and follows you along during your

70

entire search process. If you are not confident and positive about your abilities to be marketable to a company, it will show in the search process.

One of the most common reasons people get discouraged and find their confidence level diminishing is repetition—waking up every morning doing the same thing over and over again. Make sure you mix up the techniques of you job search. Do not do the same thing every day. People ask me all the time how I structure my day, and I tell them I often do not have a structure. Although I do have a foundation of what I want to accomplish, I recognize that the day will evolve depending on what actually happens during that day.

You need to take the same approach when doing your job search. Force changes in your routine to make sure that you do not feel like you are becoming stagnant. Do things to avoid falling into the trap of negativity that often is caused my long-term repetition. This thought process is often used within a company to keep an employee motivated and happy.

I remember a time when I was touring a manufacturing plant. I noticed an employee that seemed very unhappy and dissatisfied with her job. I walked up to her and started asking questions. One of the first questions I asked was, "How long have you been sitting here watching bottles go by?" Her response to me was very surprising: "22 years." I thought to myself. I would rather pull all my teeth out without Novocain, than to watch bottles go by every day for five days a week over 22 years! That was it. She did nothing else. I asked her, "If you could do something else would you be happy?" She said, "That would thrill me, but I don't think the company wants to teach me anything else."

People who are caught up in repetitive actions and events will ultimately become bored, which will be reflected in their attitude, demeanor, and productivity. Again, how you come across to companies and hiring authorities is a huge determining factor on whether a company feels you are interested and excited about an opportunity. So be careful and cognizant of your attitude and how you present yourself.

Recruiters and Job Search Agencies

A great resource that will help you not only find potential companies and employers to approach, but also customize your marketability, is working with a professional recruiter. The most common misconception candidates have is that recruiters only care about the almighty dollar. But good recruiters who have been around for many years look at their business as a brand, too. They don't want to market a product that would give them a bad reputation. So a recruiter is going to put forth a good amount of effort to make sure that you are marketed and branded in a positive way as to not only benefit them but also benefit you! A recruiter does not want to be that guy who "sells you the product that stops working after six months."

Given that a recruiter only wants to market a good product, it is critical that you are marketable to them first. This only works if you are honest, up front, and provide as much information as possible to the recruiter so they can help identify the best ways to sell you and market you to a company. The last thing you want to do is lie about your work history or recent termination merely because you are afraid the recruiter will not work with you. Instead, talk to them about your own personal circumstances, and then tell them why they still want to market you as a product to their consumer. Respect the recruiter's business and reputation by being upfront with them even if it may limit the opportunities presented to you. It's better for the recruiter and hiring committee to hear it from you than to learn about the issue through the hiring process on their own.

If you have had frequent job changes in your work history or have had problems with previous employment, it would only benefit you to tell this to your recruiter up front as to prevent issues with your relationship in the future. For example, I was told by a candidate that he was moved around so much within a company because he did so much good for the company. However, two days later I happened to be talking to an old boss of his who said this candidate had moved so much because he was not doing well as a supervisor and could not manage the teams he was tasked to manage.

As a job seeker, you need to help the recruiter better understand what you have done in your career and why you have made certain career choices so they can better market you as a potential employee. It is a lot easier convincing someone to hire an ex-jail inmate if they know and trust them than if you present yourself as just any John Doe off the street who wants employment.

You also need to be realistic in how you approach your search with a recruiter. Just because you're working with a recruiter does not mean they are going to be able to get a company to pay you twice as much. It does not mean that they are going to be able to get you that vice president job straight out of college. What it does mean is that they have abilities to help you if you have realistic expectations.

I definitely would not rely on recruiters to find you a job. I also would not recommend only working with one particular recruiter. If you are truly going to brand and sell yourself to a company for a better career opportunity, you need to take advantage of multiple avenues toward achieving this. It goes back to the wise adage of not putting all your eggs into one basket.

Getting Engaged

The only way for a brand to become more recognizable is by people using it more and more. It is the same when selling yourself to an organization. You need to focus your attention on the desire to get engaged with the organization's needs. Learn what challenges the organization is facing and how you might be able to strategize to overcome those challenges.

Companies want to know that you aren't going to be that employee that is known as "that person in the third cube on the left." Mind you, I am not saying you need to be pushy and become overly aggressive. But make sure you let a company know that if it is looking for someone to help them become more profitable and increase its sales and organizational performance, you want to be a part of those successes by getting yourself involved.

Even though the company may not have a long term succession plan for you, constantly think of how you want to impact the organization in your job 30, 60, and even 90 days out. Communicate that you are not going to allow yourself to be just an employee who "does their job." You want to be able to bring progress and growth in the organization by getting engaged and always thinking ahead.

Creating a brand for yourself has become more and more important as our technology has evolved. Think about what it was like looking for a job 20 years ago. We did not have the internet. Jobs were not posted on boards. Companies didn't have stacks of resumes to sift through. Therefore, back in the day, branding yourself was easy because there wasn't much competition. Now think about walking down the water aisle in a grocery store. There may be 7-10 different brands of water. Various sizes, labels, and pricing. But is there really that big of a difference in the taste of water?

If there were only two job candidates for companies to choose from it would be simple. But because there are thousands of resumes coming through a large company every week, it is even more critical to find ways to market yourself differently and stand out as the brand of choice.

The most critical part of marketing yourself is being flexible and agile with your marketing plan. No company or hiring authority is the same. Every company will have its own process on how they will look at and consider applicants. It is similar to dating; no two people are the same. You will always have personality differences, physical characteristics, ideology and beliefs, etc. that will differ. So it is very important to be willing to constantly and self-consciously alter your approach to marketing yourself based on the company or individual you are marketing yourself to. It is time for you to become your own brand!

Tim, a 52-year-old man who would like to improve his job before he retires, understands his lack of a degree makes the job search more challenging. He really doesn't want to change fields because he feels very satisfied and fulfilled in the manufacturing industry. So Tim decides to focus on some of the things he has learned and implemented over the last twenty years. He knows that most manufacturing companies are focusing on lean manufacturing and continuous improvement. Tim has actually completed his Black Belt certification in Six Sigma and has been project manager on implementation of several lean events. He decides to focus on his lean capabilities because they have become a valuable skill in his business. He also has operator licenses and certifications for several types of industrial equipment, which he knows can be valuable.

Tim's goals and focus is simple – target companies that focus on lean operations by highlighting his training in these areas. He also decides to join several engineering and lean organizations to start networking with folks that specialize in these areas.

Samantha's focus is now to target Brand Marketing with a Consumer Product company. Because the industry is so large, she wants to first understand the industry's trends and see where the most growth is.  During the recession, private label branding has seen a tremendous amount of opportunity. Working in the energy business, she has actually done a lot of work marketing energy solutions for third party carriers as their own product. She realizes that this type of branding is exactly what private label branding is all about.

Knowing that the private label industry is big business, she creates a portfolio of the brand marketing programs she has developed for her private third party carriers. She then decides to build a PowerPoint showing an analogy and mirror of how these programs relate to current Consumer Products and emphasize the similarities in the delivery of these programs. She also becomes involved in several online consumer product organization blogs to start communicating and networking with people in the consumer products industry to start creating a name for herself.

George wants to continue using his strengths in growing investments and values for customers. He figures out that instead of being with a company that strictly focuses on investments for consumers, he actually could take his finance experience and work behind the scenes at a company to invest the company's assets and grow its value. The biggest advantage that George has over many people in the industry is that although he worked mainly in investing client assets, most of his clients were small businesses or millionaires with diverse portfolios. He also has a CPA license, along with experience working in public and private firms.

His approach is going to be simple: he is going to highlight his success in growing the assets of his diverse group of clients and use those successes to show a company that being able to juggle a collection of clients and grow their assets would allow him to drive success in growth in the investments of a large company. He is going to build a spreadsheet showing a combined view of the assets he has invested and the growth he has made in those investments. Knowing that the industry is very network-driven; he starts joining all the local and regional finance groups and joins networking groups on the various social networking sites. He also signs up for the semi-annual finance industry investor's clinic, which is a three-day workshop where he can get involved in some of the latest investing techniques and network with senior level finance executives.

Pete, a very bright, talented, and energetic young man in his mid-twenties, knows that it is very tough for new college graduates to get jobs in their fields of study. He wants get into counseling and coaching long-term but understands that he has to start somewhere. While he was in college he was a manager at a local bar and had staff working for him. He gained a lot of experience in training and developing people. He wants to focus on some type of leadership position in a service or manufacturing field knowing that this is where his leadership skills will be the most applicable.

He really feels that he needs to continue managing people and building on his mentor and coaching experience that he has learned in the bar business. He plans to focus his resume, emphasizing his management capabilities, and starts to collect references supporting his capabilities hiring and building employees. He also knows how important teams are within companies in today's economy, so he puts together sample team-building trainings that he made during his time managing his local bar to show his capabilities creating a collaborative team.

# PERFORMING A JOB SEARCH

The first thing to remember is that 85% of the positions that exist are not published or advertised for. Why is this factor so important? Just because a position has requirements that you don't meet, or just because a company has no advertised openings, does not mean you pass the company by. The best opportunities are often those of which the public is not aware.

Why is this advantageous to the job seeker? Simple. If people do not know about it, there is less competition. It is the same reason why there are companies and recruiters that will not talk to candidates who post their resumes on a job board. People naturally do not want to be one of many being considered. It also makes it easier to focus them on what you have to offer.

So when thinking about how you are going to approach your job search, keep the hidden position in mind. Never hold back your resume and your credentials just because it may appear a need does not exist. The best example of this would be my own job search out of college. Back in 1997, when I was in college, we did not have the internet. I printed, stuffed, stamped, and mailed out 700+ resumes to companies all over the country. I did this totally randomly without even looking to see if they had an opening. My final semester I interviewed with 128 companies and received five firm job offers from companies I ultimately pursued.

The other thing you want to remember is that the potential new employer may not even realize they are missing something, that they have a need that you could fill. You must patiently, and in a professional way, teach them these things.

When engaging in a job search, there are many obvious and simple ways that you can look for a position:

- Internet searches
- Employment websites and job boards
- Facebook, LinkedIn, other social networking sites

- Newspaper or magazine advertisements
- Working with a recruitment agency
- Going to state, private, government, or publicly-funded employment services
- Job and Career fairs
- Going door-to-door (or on the phone) and ask about potential employment
- Job seeking networking groups or organizations that focus on job availability

These are ways that we consider obvious ways of performing a job search. But what are some passive ways to find opportunities?

- Sending your resume out to potential employers even though they may not have a need.
- Networking – Talking to peers, associates, friends, and family on any opportunities or connections they may have on hiring needs in the industry.
- Mass marketing – Sending your resume via mail, fax, or email to companies in a target industry or market.
- Give others access to your resume and encourage them to send your credentials to potential companies if they hear of any possible needs.
- Use yourself as a reference. Allow people to give your name as a reference for their employment, which will allow you to establish contacts within the industry you may not have had.
- Make sure you put information regarding your work / employment history on your social networking sites even if the site is catering to more social than professional networking (example Facebook vs. LinkedIn).
- Watch articles in newspapers, TV, magazines, and PR announcements. If a company announces growth, increasing in

size or adding on to their organization – this makes it a good target.

- Add yourself to newsgroups and other social network groups where you get announcements of the latest things happening in that group. Often times these will include employment or company strategic needs.
- Target companies that you are a consumer of. Do not be afraid to ask who they know higher up in the organization.
- Utilize Chat Rooms and Blogs – the more noise you make the more well-known you will become.
- Create your own website to generate traffic and interest in your skills and experiences.

Now that you have some of the active and passive ways to do a job search, it is time to dig a little deeper into some of them that are utilized but often not to the maximum potential. The most serious and common places is job boards and job search engines.

The most common reason why people are not successful in finding a job online is they are afraid to submit their resume. The most common thing I hear is "Well, the job says it requires a degree and I do not have one, so I will not submit my resume." What is one of the first things you learned about at the beginning of this chapter? Most jobs are not advertised! The other common misnomer is that just because a job says it "requires" a certain skill or experience does not mean the company won't consider your resume.

My first piece of advice, if you are interested – send your resume anyway! What is the worst that will happen? You will not get a response or hear anything. Your resume went floating off to someone's inbox and ultimately ended up in their trash. But there are so many reasons why just sending your resume can be advantageous.

When I first decided to search for a job and change employers back in the late 90's, I sent my resume out to different companies and recruiters around the local area. One of the recruiting agencies that got my resume decided to call me to do a pre-screen to see if they had any possible jobs for me and where they could place me. When the manager called me up to have a conversation with me, halfway through the conversation she asked me if I ever thought of being a recruiter.

Of course my first immediate reaction to her question was, No. I did not want or have any desire to get into a commission sales position. I was more interested in finding some type of sales supervisor or retail position managing people. But for whatever reason she was stuck on wanting me to be a recruiter.

After weeks of courting, and quite frankly her annoying persistence, I decided to take a leap of faith and take her up on her offer. Twelve years later, I am one of the top performing recruiters in the country. The point to my story is that I never would have considered getting into recruiting if my resume did not fall into her hands. It happened for a reason. It happened by fate. Would I have ever applied for the job if it was advertised? No. But she saw more in my resume and on the phone then I did. So she took a chance.

There are so many ways you can utilize the internet for doing a job search. So I would like to take some time covering some of the most widely used and most valuable resources; starting with internet job boards.

Internet Job Boards

There are many different internet job board sites that can be found throughout the internet. Sites that, in many instances, will focus on a particular industry, level of job, types of employment, or broad band sites that focus on the masses. Utilizing these sites can be very helpful in not only finding a job, but also establishing long-term contacts and additional knowledge about the trends in the industry you are targeting.

The first rule when posting your resume on a job board is to make sure you put as much attention to detail in posting your profile and your resume as you did writing your resume itself. One of the biggest mistakes that I have found people make is that when they upload, type, or import their resume onto a job board site they forget to check for bad formatting, misspellings, and grammatical imperfections.

How you represent yourself, especially the first impressions, can be a critical aspect to getting to the next step in the process. So you want to make sure whatever resume you are using on the boards best represents you and how you want to market or brand yourself. Many websites allow you to upload your actual Word version of you resume, at the same time keeping your formatting. This is great. This is ideal because you do not really have to change anything.

Other websites do not allow you to import your resume and strip the formatting when you import them. This takes a little more attention to detail. You need to go through and make sure you spell check the resume and make sure there are no errors in the transition. Verify the dates of employment and the work history because often times this is an area that can become jumbled or altered. It is critical to not change or be mistaken on dates of employment. When dates are not accurate, people assume it was done to deceive the employer. Also check the formatting. Take a view of what the profile and resume looks like to a future employer. Is this how you want to market yourself?

There are two ways you can list a potential resume on a job board: you can list an active resume that exposes all your contact information and present employment information, or you can have a confidential resume where you keep hidden your personal information and current employer. Make sure if you are uploading a confidential resume that you change the document name to a generic name (don't leave it first initial, last name . doc), and also make sure you take out any company identifiers in the resume.

Company identifiers are company-specific titles, phrases, acronyms or words that would reveal to a potential employer who you are currently working for. That means that you may have to alter your current job title to a more generic title so that it does not disclose or hint at who your current job is with. Also remember to remove product indicators, brand names, etc. from the text so as not to expose your search.

The next step in utilizing a job board site is actually searching and applying for jobs. Most sites will not only allow you to easily and readily forward your resume to a future employer, but it will often times reveal the email address or contact information of the company representative as well. Why is this important? It is much more professional and you are better likely to get the attention of a prospective employer if you email them a copy of your resume as an attachment versus going through the boards. Do not get me wrong; if you have to go through the board you have to. It is perfectly acceptable. It just would be better if given the accessibility of their contact information that you send it as a personalized email instead.

Make sure you send your resume, even if you think they may already have it or they may not think you are qualified. While you may not be a particular fit for a job that is posted or listed on the job site, your resume could still float into the hands of a hiring manager who takes great interest in your background.

As a reminder to those planning to post resumes on various job sites, keep a record of where you post your resume. Make sure it stays updated and refreshed. If your job search changes in any way, update these sites to reflect the changes. The other major thing you want to remember is when you get a job; take your resume down from the sites! Do not leave your resume posted on job boards if you do not want people to solicit you further for opportunities. Also, make sure that if you have set up job search agents that you update them when things change and delete them when you find a job.

Job Search Sites

Another way to utilize the internet is to go onto job search sites that will search multiple websites at a given time to identify potential positions for you. This is also known as spider searching. When you go on these sites, it will pull from thousands of company websites, search engines, job boards, etc. to retrieve results that best match the search criteria you're looking for.

It would be more effective to take the results you get and contact the company directly via email, fax, or mail than go through the third party provider or the domain. The only exceptions to this are with companies that require you to set up a profile on its actual company website and submit your resume that way. Companies that require you to do this are creating a database of applicants that apply for their jobs. This way if they do not have a position that is presently available that fits your background, they still have access to your resume in the future if their needs change. Taking the time to go on an employer-based job seekers site and filling out a profile is mutually beneficial for both parties long-term.

Internet Networking

Online networking through news groups, association sites, and social networking groups are also great ways to hear about, apply for, and network for a job. Companies often peruse these sites, talking about immediate job needs, hiring initiatives, or future growth plans that would enable you to establish contacts for the future. The thing you should always keep in mind is that posts you make are public. Be careful how you approach posting on these sites and make sure not to disclose information that you want to remain confidential.

Newspapers/Magazines

There are also many websites that take a collaborative look at newspaper posting nationwide.  As you know, physical newspapers have become nearly obsolete. Perhaps you frequently find yourself searching the newspapers' online classified sections for positions rather than actually picking up a hard copy of the newspaper or magazine. There are websites that have taken the initiative of bringing search results of all these newspapers together into one site so as to make it easier to make information more accessible.

## Education and Employer Alumni Sites

These are other fantastic ways of networking, especially for long-term goals of employment. When you join these sites there are typically no restrictions on how long you can stay on these sites. It is a great way to keep in touch with past peers, managers, and contacts that you have made in the industry. It can also provide a great avenue for finding people for potential references if needed.

## Resume Marketing Sites

There are several sites available that send out your resume to thousands of potential employers for a minimal cost. I do not typically recommend these sites, however. As a recruiter who looks at resumes every day, when I see a resume that comes from one of these mass blastings I typically just delete them. Many times the resume has nothing to do with anything that I work on or have any affiliation with. Hence, using these sites makes it hard to know your target audience.

## Social Media Sites

There are many creative and industrial ways of utilizing these sites, many of which can help people in their career searches. I have dedicated a whole chapter to social media and networking for this very reason.

Utilizing the internet is going to be one of the most important ways for a person to find a position today, and especially in the future. The number of companies that are actively using the internet to search for employees is estimated to increase by 20 times over the next 2-3 years. This is where the technology is going and where employers are looking for people.

## Networking

Lastly, the third most popular and beneficial way to seek employment is through networking. You can network with everyone in your life. It can be friends, family, coworkers, members of associations, and even the person you sit next to on a plane. Networking can be with anyone to whom you can introduce yourself and describe your marketable skills.

The most important thing to remember when networking is to make sure the other person knows your intent. What are you looking for and what do you need from that person? Make sure they understand what your needs are and are able to keep their eyes open for opportunities that may match those needs.

Talk to your contact. Get to know them. Learn from them. Often times the person you are networking with can give you insight into their world and the accessibility of people that could help you in achieving your career goals. Do not be afraid to ask questions and learn about the person's current work environment. The more information you obtain about their employment, the more information you'll feel comfortable sharing with them about your employment goals. And the more they learn about your employment goals, the better connected they will be to you and your goals.

When networking with a person, make sure to write down and follow-up on any referrals that this person gives to you. The worst thing you can do is not follow-up on a job lead or referral. It diminishes your credibility. It shows that you are not truly serious about furthering your search and reaching your goals. People will stop trying to help you and will not want to pass your name along to others. Do not lose your credibility. Get the email address of each referral. Setup a template email for follow-ups thanking the people for their time, and follow-up with a cover letter and a resume. Use the template every time you receive a referral through your networking efforts.

Create a list of target companies or types of opportunities that you are trying to engage in. Use this list as the basis for how you network with others. This does not mean you have to stick to your list, but make an effort to make contacts that can help you penetrate companies and opportunities that are on your list. Making a list gives you the ability to create goals. Goals are the key to being successful in any job search.

By utilizing job boards and networking, you can easily delve into new opportunities that will ultimately lead to achieving your short- and long-term goals. These are not the only methods of looking for a job, but these are the foundation for any successful job search.

Tim knows that the manufacturing industry advertises quite a bit of opportunities online and in trade magazines. This is going to be Tim's primary focus in looking for opportunities. He also is going to branch out online and start joining several manufacturing industry websites and check the job boards to see what openings are available. Tim realizes that not having a degree is a major challenge, so he is focusing on quantity. Getting his name out into the market will increase his chances at finding job leads.

Samantha is focusing on the Consumer Products industry. This industry is all about trade shows and landscaping their innovative marketing initiatives and branding strategies. She signs up for several large industry expos and functions to do meet-and-greets and network with prospective employers. This is where much of the industry finds and recruits new talent. Networking is key here. She also hits the job boards and LinkedIn to see where companies have the largest Brand Management needs; she'll focus her applications to these areas. She recognizes there are numerous openings, so finding a job is not going to be the hard part; selling her skills and abilities are going to be the key.

George starts his search by contacting local finance associations in his area and talking to the association's presidents and board representatives. He starts the process of getting referrals to possible companies that may have an interest in an investment manager. George has created his own website and has built up his different social networking sites to emphasize his background in growing investments. He then creates his network by joining groups online and adding members to his network to start getting his name out. The types of jobs that George is going to be targeting is not going to be through a recruitment agency or job boards; he knows he'll have to get leads and focus on back-end networking to make connections at prospective companies.

Pete is just graduating college and has only some work experience while he was getting his degree. For Pete, it's important to get his name out there. He starts working with his college's career office to apply for jobs that are posted by companies at his college. He also decides to go online and start sending out his resume via email to various large companies in the local market as well as other markets that he would be interested in relocating to. He is not necessarily focusing on posted jobs; he specifically is focusing on companies he feels he can enjoy working for. Although he still explores the job boards to look for entry-level positions, Pete spends most of his time calling companies and sending his resume directly to companies' HR and hiring managers, even if a job isn't posted. He wants to forgo the competition by finding a company that wants someone but hasn't officially started to search.

# RECRUITERS

Another popular method of job searching, often times for active and passive candidates, is working with a recruiter. Interviewing and building a relationship with a recruiter can completely change the dynamic of your job search. Candidates may think of recruiters as sales people merely looking to make money. Sure, recruiters do make money; they are performing a service and getting paid for it. But there are a lot of driving factors behind a recruiter. Some of these factors are motivated in your favor, others are not. A good recruiter realizes the balance between the candidate and company and make sure both parties achieve a common goal. However, if you are not paying the recruiter, and the company is, then you have to be a little prepared and guarded on his or her motivations.

Motivations can vary and have a lot of short-term and long-term results. The most common motivation is money. But, there are many others.

Here are some examples of common motivations:

- Having an established, long-term relationship with the recruiter could reap tremendous benefits in the future. For instance, if a recruiter places you within a company at a lower level and you stay with the company for the next 20-30 years, the recruiter has a likely chance to work with you as a hiring authority. It is because of this that recruiters create a value in the relationship he/she has with you.
- If a recruiter has worked with other recruiters in the past then they understand the difficulties, challenges, and advantages of dealing with such a person. They tend to have a more invested interest of the relationship that they are developing with you and take a greater value in this relationship.
- Recruiters typically have created valued relationships with companies that have value dividends in the long-term. For the recruiter to maintain such a strong relationship with a

company and truly take that relationship to a superior level they want to make sure every person they place is a success story. If they place someone with a company that is not the right match and that person ends up leaving the organization then there is a negative impact on that relationship.

- When a recruitment agency is working on a retained search, they have an exclusive relationship with the company and are usually paid prior to the placement even occurring. This is advantageous to the candidate for many reasons. Because the recruiter has already been paid, they will not look at the candidate as a paycheck but will focus on the fulfillment of the job. Since the recruiter has an exclusive on the position you do not have to worry about other agencies representing candidates to the job, which would decrease your chances for the position.

- Many recruiters actually do care about what they do and who they place. It is not just about the dollars and cents. Often times recruiters who have been in the business for 10+ years are more motivated by building relationships than by anything else. For them, the money is a secondary benefit and reward that comes from placing the right people with the right client.

- Recruiters get paid more in fees when they get you more money. If a recruiter can get you $100K when you are only looking for $90K, the recruiter will get it for you. The recruiter will get a higher payout and you will be getting more money. Just because you know that the recruiter is getting paid, doesn't mean his only motivation is getting "something." He wants to improve your situation as much as possible so that his situation will improve as much as possible.

Working with recruiters can have tremendous benefits and they can have tremendous disadvantages.

Advantages:

- Frequently searches that are offered are exclusive to recruitment agencies only.
- Recruiters are your personal advocate and cheerleader. This individual is your best tool for selling and marketing yourself to a company.
- Recruiters have built and developed relationships with companies around the country and can use these relationships to help prospective candidates be considered for potential positions.
- With the increasing unemployment rate, companies are overwhelmed with more and more résumés. Companies are starting to turn to recruiters to weed through the stacks of résumés and narrow them down to the top candidates for any particular position.
- If you are trying to do a job search confidentially or while you are working full-time, recruiters can be tremendously helpful in keeping your search confidential while actively seeking out employers for you to entertain for a potential career change.
- Maintaining confidentiality during your job search is difficult when searching on your own. Using a recruiter helps you look into the available market without being fully exposed.
- Recruiters have a tremendous knowledge base of the target company that you are interviewing with. They can give you background, needs, and profiles of the company that will help you engage them on the solutions they need.
- When you allow a recruiter to negotiate an offer for you, it is much easier for them to negotiate the compensation and other

aspects of the offer without creating a bad feeling or image between you and the company.

Disadvantages:

- Like most of us, recruiters are motivated by potential financial gains.
- Companies seldom want to pay the cost to hire a recruiting agency. Because of this cost, many positions are not accessible to agencies.
- Recruiters can be difficult to reach by phone, and even by email, they get thousands of calls and résumés every week.
- Companies are the ones that hire the recruiters. Therefore, the recruiters often are working for the best interest of the companies rather than candidates.
- Recruiters may limit your access to other positions when they are seriously considering you for a position. The biggest reason for this is to control your interests in the one job and not create uncertainty on which one you will take. So while the position you are entertaining with the recruiter may be a good opportunity, the opportunity the recruiter is withholding may be the better opportunity for you.

If you choose to work with recruiters, there are definitely things you need to know to make it advantageous for you. There are also professional courtesies that you should honor when working with a recruiter or agency. Remember, not only does the recruiter/agency work for the company that hired them, but they also have a lot of influence over other companies that could possibly entertain you as an applicant.

So while you may have hostility over the fact the recruiter is actually getting paid if you take the job, you need to try to keep a focused and open relationship with the recruiter. Good recruiters truly hold a lot of the cards.

There have been several occasions in my years in the industry where I have actually told a company, "Please do not offer the candidate the job because I do not feel he/she is a fit for your organization, and I will not guarantee the success of this hire."

Although it is rare when a recruiter takes this action, it does happen. This is driven by the concerns that if the recruiter places the candidate with the company, there are going to be problems or issues. Recruiters do not want unsuccessful hires on their records. The last thing they want is a candidate that goes to work for a company and fails to meet the needs of the company or, even worse, they become a human resources problem.

Get out of your mind the idea that you are only a fee to the recruiter. Certainly do not approach a recruiter in that fashion. You need to give the recruiter a chance to work through your needs and try to help you not only get what you are looking for but be your cheerleader in getting the position. Work toward making a win-win situation for both you and the recruiter.

Supplying Important Information

An important thing to remember is you need to supply as much information to the recruiter as possible. It is in your best interest to be honest, and you certainly should make sure you think about which details you plan to provide to the recruiter before getting on the phone with them.

The following are examples of what recruiters need to know:
- Are you presently employed?
- If yes, what is your primary motivation for your job search?
- Tell me a little about your company; what's the purpose of the operation? What products and services are involved? Are they private, public, national or regional?
- Who are some of the biggest competitors of your present (most recent) employer?

- What are the main responsibilities of your job and how many people do you support within your department?
- What is your typical day like and what is your current schedule? What are your expectations in your next position and how flexible can you be with your schedule and travel?
- What are the top three elements you feel you are missing in your currently role that you would like to see in your new position?
- What technical skills or training/certifications have you acquired during your career?
- Do you enjoy your current job environment, and if not, why not?
- How do you feel about relocation?
- Have you discussed relocation with important members in your family and have you researched the location you are considering?
- How soon are you available for a phone interview, in-person interview, and to start at the new company?
- What is your current or more recent base salary? What are your expectations on salary in your next position?
- What are some of your biggest motivations in your career?
- Rank the following factors in order of most important to least important: benefits, money, location, advancement, challenges, and job security.
- What have you already done to find a job?
- Who have you interviewed with in the last three months? Who have you already submitted your résumé to?
- What has been the feedback from the jobs you have already interviewed with?
- What is the best way to contact you and do you have any alternative contacts such as cell phone or work phone?

Be Honest. Do not lie to the person that is representing you. The last thing you want to do is be dishonest. You need to give the recruiter as much information about yourself, situation, and needs in order for them to help you most effectively. By withholding information you are not only hurting your relationship with the recruiter, but you are making it hard for the recruiter to help you obtain the job you want.

Salary

Be realistic about your salary expectations. Be honest with the recruiter about all the salary and benefits you are getting in your current role and what it is going to take for you to change jobs. Stand by your word. Do not commit to a salary only to back out at the end.

If a recruiter asks you, "What will it take for you to take the job?" and you give the recruiter an actual value or number, you need to stand by your word. Being honest will help you be consistent with the recruiter and the company. Nothing upsets a recruiter more than you telling them one number and then in the interview telling the company another. If there are going to be other important factors that will influence your ultimate decision in addition to this number, communicate this to the recruiter before they start negotiating on your behalf. These factors may be benefits, vacation, schedule, or a combination of a variety of factors. Talk about everything you are considering that goes in to the number you are quoting. The last thing you want to do is surprise the recruiter by turning the job down after they have negotiated the ideal job offer with the salary, vacation, schedule, etc. that you told them you wanted.

Consider why you would change jobs. Make sure you tell the recruiter exactly why you might consider switching jobs or careers. Tell them exactly what you are looking for in a career move, and what you do not want in a company. Create a clear picture. The clearer the picture you paint for the recruiter, the more success they will have matching you with the right opportunity. Being unsure and vague will only cause problems with your relationship and ability to decide on what to pursue down the road.

## Activity/Interviews

Make sure you communicate with your recruiter on all the active interviews you have and the opportunities you are pursuing. If a recruiter talks to you about a specific opportunity, let him know if you believe you have already been presented. Even though you think your resume has been presented to the company, the recruiter can make sure and present you if not. But if you lie to the recruiter about being presented, and he ends up finding out that you have, it will damage your relationship with the recruiter.

If you have an opportunity that you are leaning toward, or have an extreme interest in, and it conflicts with the opportunity the recruiter represents, do not be afraid to tell the recruiter. The recruiter needs to know what they are up against. The recruiter has a right to know. The recruiter then can either provide you with the information needed to make the best decision possible, or they can look into opportunities that may better suit your needs.

## Relocation

Lastly, the most common issue that comes up when working with a recruiter that causes problems with the relationship you are developing comes down to a job that involves relocation. Talk to your family and know your true availability to relocate before working with a recruiter or an agency. Do not start working with a recruiter if you are uncertain about relocating. It is not fair to anyone to make them believe you have a sincere interest in a role when you have not gotten clarity on this subject.

A common problem in our business is when a candidate tells a recruiter they are open to relocation or have no geographic restrictions, when they have not even told their wife that they are actually looking for a job. Recruiters will ask you whether you have had a conversation with your spouse or any other important parties in your life that will influence your ability to relocate. It is extremely important for you to be honest and not tell the recruiter what you think he or she wants to hear. If you are upfront with them, it will only make the process easier for everyone.

Also, make sure you research an area that a recruiter is suggesting when looking at an opportunity. If the recruiter approaches you about a location and you are unsure if it fits your needs, research the area before going through the process. Do not wait until you receive an offer to decide that you need to figure out whether the location is right for you.

An example of this came when I was working on a high level regional management position with one of my biggest company clients. Several times throughout the process I asked the candidate if he had talked to his family (wife and kids) about the relocation process and had fully discussed and cleared moving to the new location. The candidate insisted that there were no issues with regards to relocation. This candidate went through two phone interviews, three in-person interviews, a costly psychological assessment, and months of process. When the offer was presented to the candidate it exceeded all his expectations that he had when he originally started the process. A day after he received the offer, just when I thought the candidate was going to accept the job, I got the call.

"I'm really excited about the opportunity, and I am very happy with the offer. It's a very generous offer. However, I have a small issue. My wife is very concerned about the area and really isn't sure it's the right place for our family. Family is very important to me, and I can't put my family through this if they won't be happy."

After lengthy discussions with the candidate, I found out the biggest concern that the wife had with this location was the school systems. He and his wife had raised their family in a very conservative Christian home. They had three girls that were in their teens going to private Christian schools. She was tremendously concerned about moving to the area and being able to provide her daughters the environment that would continue to support their traditional values and goals for their family.

I was devastated. The candidate insisted that he was going to do the research with his wife before making a firm commitment. But I did not let that stop me from doing my own research. I contacted dozens of candidates and contractors I had in the location of the new job and started gathering information on the school systems in the area. Surprisingly, not only did the location have a very strong Christian school system, but one of the largest companies that helps develop and build up the population of the area was a very Christian company. One of the contacts I had in the area made a comment that to this day I haven't forgotten: "Michael, there are four pews for every person in our community. You can't get more Christian than that."

As I acquired information about this relocation, I was disseminating it to the candidate and his wife to review. I was confident that with all the feedback and information I was able to give to the applicant, he would call me after the weekend to determine a start date.

Then, on Sunday night as I was relaxing at home, the unbelievable happened. It came as an email that the candidate was rejecting the offer. The reason, he claimed, had to do with his inability to ignore his family needs when making a move. I was completely baffled.

Normally I would pick up the phone or send an email and argue with the candidate. But I had done everything I could to get the information to the candidate that he needed. So using the advice of one of my mentors, I decided to ignore him. I told the company he had rejected the offer and we needed to pursue other candidates. They were completely devastated and confused. They wanted him. But there was nothing I could do at this point.

Two days later I received an email from the candidate. The letter was very emotional. He was deeply sorry for the decision that he made and for many days after he was regretting how he concluded this search. He was begging me to get him the job back. With a little conversation and a lot of charm we were able to get the offer put back on the table and the deal was done. That did not stop me from asking the candidate what exactly caused him to write that email.

"When my middle child approached me and told me she didn't want to move, I reacted." I could tell he was passionate about family and making sure that everyone in his family had an opportunity to be a part of the decision. But after several days of talking and stewing, they all agreed that the move was the right decision.

Being honest with your recruiter and telling them everything that is going on can save a lot of time, money, and energy spent pursuing something that just will not work. Had this candidate talked to his wife and kids before the interview process even started, he could have avoided the embarrassment of this process and it would have occurred a lot smoother. The only negative that could have occurred is if he did not do the due diligence at the beginning. If he just did a cursory view of the location and said that he was not interested, then he may never have known how great this move would have been.

So make sure whether it is relocation, salary, shift, hours, work environment, or any other matters that may involve your family – talk to your family! Be honest with the recruiter on the conversations you're having with the important people in your life and what the challenges are. Even the recruiter might be able to help resolve issues that may seem almost impossible to solve.

Other Basic Questions

There are many other questions that a recruiter will ask you and highlight when trying to determine a fit and how they can help you.

Here is a more thorough overview of questions you can expect:
- Why are you looking? What brings you to the job market today?
- What is your current salary and what are your salary expectations for your next position?
- Do you get paid any extra incentives related to your salary including bonuses, commissions, or paid overtime?
- How far are you willing to commute for a position?
- Are you willing to relocate?

- Have you discussed relocation with the people that are important to the relocation?
- What areas of the country are you willing to consider when relocating for a job?
- Will you go to a small town in the middle of nowhere or a large metro city like Los Angeles/New York City? What type of demographic or population requirements do you have when looking at an area?
- What level of education have you completed?
- What schools did you obtain your degree(s) from? Was this an online program or did you physically go to a school campus to get your degree? Was this an accredited school?
- Tell me more about what you do in your current role and in previous roles.
- What would you say are your top three things you are considering when looking at your next position?
- What do you like the most and the least about your current job?
- Are you open to work different hours and alternative work week schedules? This can include working shift work (nights) or working the weekend schedule.
- Do you have union or non-union experience?
- Do you like working for larger or smaller companies, or does the size of the company not really play a factor in your decision?
- How soon are you available for a phone interview?
- How much notice do you need to do a face-to-face interview?
- Are you working with other recruiters or search firms?
- Where are you at with other interviews and potential offers?
- Which companies have you already interviewed with? You do NOT want a recruiter to send your résumé to a place you have already applied to. It can be tremendously damaging to your ability to get a job with that company.

- Do you have any special family needs that will be important and affect your schedule or relocation on your next position?
- Do you currently own a home? If yes, what have you done to look in to selling your home and what will it take to sell it?
- Do you have any unique skills that you think will be considered valuable to a future employer?
- Are you a legal US Citizen, Green Card Holder, or Permanent Resident? Do you require sponsorship?

## Value Recruiter's Coaching

When working with a recruiter during the entire recruiting process you need to listen, absorb, and value what that person is telling you. Most of what the recruiter tells you are going to help you perform better in the interview process, and will actually help in your overall interviewing abilities and career goals in general.

The recruiter coaches you through the process, not only to make sure you have the necessary things you need to do well, but the recruiter is also trying to level the playing field between you and the company. When you work directly with the company they are not going to tell you exactly what they are looking for. They are going to tell you what they want you to know.

Recruiters are great because they will give you the inside story and a view of what to expect. Often times they can tell you why other people did not get the job and coach you on questions that may be asked and how to answer them. Whenever I work with a candidate on an opportunity, I always give them feedback on why other candidates were rejected so they can plan to highlight and demonstrate their skills and experiences in these areas when talking about their background. This is helpful because if you do not know that the company is going to ask behavioral questions, or that the company wants someone that is going to be team-based versus strong-minded, then you really do not know what approach to take.

Throughout the process take notes from your conversation from the recruiter. Understand that although the recruiter may know his or her client well, they are not the company. They do not work there and they cannot guarantee the style of the environment, how you will feel when working there, or whether there are growth opportunities within the company. You still need to take the time to interview the company. The only person that can uncover the pros and cons you would experience as an employee of an organization is you.

You definitely do not want to rely on other people's views on the company, even if they already worked there. What if the guy that is telling you the company was horrible to work for was fired because he had poor attendance? This person's opinion of the company is partial. They do not truly understand what the company can do for you. So interviewing the company and the people that you are going to be working for and with will be the only way to gain this knowledge. Be prepared. I will talk about interviewing the company later on in future chapters.

Understanding Closing Tactics

There are two ways to view closing tactics. One can take the ignorant view that the recruiter is trying to take control of the process and force you to take a position you are not going to be happy with. Or you can take a positive view of the closing process: that the recruiter is simply trying to take the emotion out of your decision and peel away the skin to get to the hard facts.

Recruiters want you to think level-headed. Most candidates get very emotional in the interviewing and offer process. They allow those emotions to get the best of them and start making decisions or react without thought. Do not take a recruiter's closing tactics as being overly aggressive or an attempt to force you into a job. Take it to your advantage. The information that you share together will allow a recruiter to maximize his or her abilities to get you the job you want with the pay you had hoped for.

There are many aggressive approaches that recruiters will take to "close the deal" and get things wrapped up. Understand the purpose of these approaches and ultimately why they are going to benefit you.

- <u>If/Then Closing</u> is the most common method of closing in our business. This is when the recruiter asks you, "If I get you $60K, then can I accept the job on your behalf?" This is not a tactical way of forcing you to take the job. They just want your commitment. If you tell them a number, be prepared to move forward if they get it for you. Do not tell them you want $60K and then when they get you $60K, or even more, you say, "I need to think about it." They probably have already accepted the job for you and the company is ready to move forward. So be committed to your decision.

- <u>If/Then Closing with Competition</u> is similar to the If/Then close but they are adding a factor in the close. They are making you aware that there are multiple candidates of interest to them but they are leaning toward making you an offer. By giving the recruiter your commitment and even a number that you will accept, the recruiter can go back and show the hiring manager that you are committed to accepting the job. Again, respect your recruiter and honor your commitment.

- <u>Hard Close</u> is when a recruiter basically calls you up and tells you that you got the job and asks you when you can start. They push you hard for a commitment even before giving you the offer details. This is often used when a candidate is honest and has communicated something to the effect of, "No matter what, I want this job." Understand that the recruiter is not trying to bully you, but they are putting the focus on the fact that you already committed to the job in as much as the details are reasonable. They will take salary and emotion out of the process.

- Take-Away can be viewed as an aggressive tactic by a recruiter to force you to commit to something that you do not want. Sure, that view has some truth to it. But, more importantly, they are trying to get you to focus on the situation and not the distractions that are causing you to be unsure of your decision. When a recruiter tells you "If you don't want the job, that's fine; I'll just tell the company to hire the other guy," he is trying to get you to stop mulling around and focus on what you truly want and why you went through this process. Look at it as going to yoga and focusing your mind. He wants all the outside distractions to be taken away so you can see the clear picture.

Understand the closing process is not designed to force you into a job; it is designed to help you understand the dynamics of your decision and get to the final answer. It can be stressful, and often seem like the recruiter is motivated by nothing other than money. But at the end of the process you will realize how emotionally cleansing the process will be. Once the dust settles and the smoke clears, you will see you made a decision for the right reasons and without any outside forces making you do it.

The relationship between a recruiter and a candidate is exactly that – a relationship. It is not a monetary transaction. It is not a "deal." It is a relationship that both parties need to value.

Since Tim is looking to remain in the manufacturing industry and wants to continue to use what he specializes in toward his career goals, he decides the best avenue would be to focus his search with recruiters. There are many recruiters that specialize in manufacturing recruitment, and he knows that the recruiters will have the capabilities to leverage him into organizations even though he doesn't have a degree. He decides to contact several regional and manufacturing specialized recruitment agencies to get their help in getting his search to be successful.

After doing extensive research, Samantha finds out that a high concentration of marketing and brand management positions are listed through executive agencies along with the job boards. She signs up and places her résumé on many of the job boards, but also contacts several executive agencies to see what retained or contingency searches they have that she would be a fit for. Although she likely could find a position online, she knows that the industry is competitive, and that executive agencies would have a better chance to get her in front of the hiring authority.

George has to do whatever he can to locate a position. He knows that a lot of recruitment agencies will have a hard time helping him because he has been out of work for a long time.  But he decides to send his résumé to every agency he can. It is no benefit to George to hold back on sending his résumé out. Many of the agencies he sends his résumé to likely will be discarded or put in a stack, so he knows that he just needs to push his information in front of everyone to get people to help him.

Pete calls around to several agencies to see if they work with entry-level college graduates. Unfortunately most agencies do not. He does find out though that the ones that do often times have job fairs and also post a lot of jobs online to attract entry-level candidates. Pete decides to focus his search online but understands that if an agency advertises for an entry-level candidate that it would be good for him to apply for the job.

# SOCIAL NETWORKING

Social Networking has become one of the biggest parts of our personal and professional life today. There are hundreds of different types of social networking and conversational websites that allow users to interact with other users. These sites allow people to network with people for reasons of all facets.

The most important thing to be mindful of when being involved in social media and social networking is that you are exposing your life to other people.  You must be willing to accept the perceptions people have when they see your profiles and posts on these networking sites. You also need to be prepared on how that can affect how you are viewed in the professional world, and even in your job search.

One of the best examples I can give is in reference to a former fellow-employee. Several months after she was hired with our company, we started to notice that she was misspelling quite a bit of words, using words in the wrong context, and that her grammar did not make sense. The first thing management did was go to her "profile page" on one of these social networking sites to discover that these errors were not merely typos. Her profile was riddled with misspelled words and grammatical errors, which proved to be a very negative portrayal of her as a person.

How does your profile or page effect how people view you?  Before we went to her page, we assumed that the errors she was making were typos. After seeing her page and understanding who she really was, we realized that she was poorly educated and hence it was pouring over into her work performance. I admit it was wrong of us to judge her based on her writing proficiency or anything viewed on a social networking site, but the truth is that people who have influence over your career will judge you based on such things. Ultimately the company took no action, but this is a leading example of how sites can affect the way people view you.

It is a growing fact that hiring authorities, peers, subordinates, and employees of all nature are using social networking access to view the profiles of current and future employees to judge and determine that person's involvement in their organization. It is because of this that it is critical for you to be more conservative with your profiles and public posts. Is what you see on your page or posts going to negatively impact your search? How will people view you?

Before using social networking sites to help you in your job search, you need to comb through them. Make sure that you have created a profile and an image that you want people to see and can respect. Use your abilities to customize your profile to create the image you want others to see. This can be helpful in not only giving people access to more information about you as a potential employee, but it can also help you further brand and market yourself.

Once you have created a profile that will maximize your abilities and create a positive and rewarding perception of who you are, it is time to utilize these sites to get your name out there and find the opportunities that will further your career goals.

Before you can truly take advantage of social networking sites, you need to create goals for what you are looking to accomplish. The first step is to build a list of potential companies that you want to target. Create a short list. Do the necessary research and determine what companies you think would be the most beneficial to progress your career.

Now that you have determined a short list of companies that you are interested to work for, go on these sites to start finding people that work for these companies. Look to see what organizations and associations some of the key players in the organizations belong to. Get involved. Join organizations, groups, and associations that these people actively involve themselves with so you can be seen. This is what we call indirect marketing.

If a target company hiring manager belongs to the same groups that you belong to, then he or she can see your interest in topics and visions of the future needs of the industry or the topic of the group. Make your presence known. Give yourself a name. Get involved in group topics. As you get more involved in groups and associations, these managers will start noticing your involvement and who you are. Your name will become recognizable. People will start seeing your mind set and how you approach situations and topics.

Approach managers you have identified at some of your target companies and create a conversation. Break the ice with this person. The most important thing you can do is show interest in that manager's knowledge. Ask about their job, the company, the goals and vision of the organization. Talk to the person about how they got to where they are at in their career. How did they get a position within the company and progress to the point of being in their current role? The key to this technique is that you do not want to just come out and tell the manager your intentions. This has become a secondary goal. Your primary goal is to get the manager's interest in talking to you and getting to know you as a person.

Once you have established some credibility and interest with the manager, you have an opportunity to take a step forward. Inquire about your desire to get with a company where you can drive and impact the bottom line. Talk about your desire to create successes as did the manager you are speaking with. Relate to this person you are talking to. Find parallels in your backgrounds and how you both have progressed your career.

As you become more comfortable and feel you are on a more personal level, you will have an opportunity to inquire about employment with the company. This does not mean you be too direct and just ask, "Does your company have any openings that they would consider me for?" Be subtle about it. Talk about how you can see the enthusiasm and excitement the manager seems to have about his or her current employer, and how you would love to have an opportunity to be a part of that. Then ask how a person like you would go about getting in with the organization.

One of the best ways to be seen or heard by a manager is by understanding the needs of the company, and using your branding techniques and marketing skills learned in the prior chapters to show a benefit to the manager. If the manager feels you have skills, experiences, and expertise that will benefit his or her organization then they are more apt to help you. Brand yourself to them. Get them to see the benefits you could bring to the organization, ultimately driving them to pursue you instead of you pursuing them.

The key to successful use of social networking goes back to successfully branding yourself. So focus your profile like you would your résumé. Make sure you are marketing and promoting the skills, strengths, and experiences that you bring to the table that would make you that much more valuable.

Next, let us take an inside look at some of the more popular social networking websites and how you can use these websites to maximize your exposure. Remember that there are hundreds of websites and apps available for job searching. The list below is only a sampling of the more popular sites.

LinkedIn

For a number of years now this site has been underutilized. But more and more companies, recruiters, and job seekers are now using this site to interact with organizations and companies in efforts to better their job searches. You can use this site to respond to job postings, engage with hiring managers of companies, and even to find and engage with recruiters that specialize in your field.

Creating a profile is key. It is very easy for you to create a profile and it be listed as complete. This is presently one of the biggest mistakes people make when starting out on LinkedIn. Too little information leads to limited responses and lack of interest. Treat your LinkedIn profile as a résumé and interview. When a person views your LinkedIn profile, they should have a full experience of who you are and the things that you bring to the table.

LinkedIn profiles allow you to highlight not only your work experience, but it also allows you to highlight your education, associations you are affiliated with, groups that you belong to, references people can write on your behalf, and even follow your activities on the site.

Join groups! LinkedIn has specialty groups that cover almost any area of work or industry. Here is the key to joining groups. You are limited to how many groups you can belong to, so pick well. Focus on groups that have a large amount of members to get the most general exposure. Make sure when joining these groups you elect to receive email updates and newsletters. Often times these announcements include job postings and hiring initiatives. Make sure to check your groups often. Many times there are free job posting sections in these groups with leads to a lot of job postings that are publicized.

Contacting people on LinkedIn is limited to people you know or that you have a direct LinkedIn connection to. There is also a great benefit with LinkedIn where you can be introduced to people within your network. If someone is not currently a contact of yours but you want to contact them, you can simply request that one of your primary LinkedIn contacts introduce you two. Not only does it credit the person that provided the lead, but it also allows managers and recruiters not to be overwhelmed by random emails.

Another great way to use the site, even if you cannot contact on the site itself, is to view some information of people, such as their names and the companies they work for. Use that information to send an email to them directly at the company. Searching a company's information on the internet is easy. You will also find out how they format their email addresses.

Facebook

Similar to LinkedIn, this site allows you to build profiles and track your daily life and passion. Although this site definitely caters more to a person's social life, you can actually create a profile that is strictly geared toward business and business initiatives (work life).

Most companies have created some type of Facebook page. This allows you not only to become friends with the company's Facebook page, but it also allows you direct, unrestricted access to anyone's page that is friends with the company, which can often include managers, hiring authorities, and even some executives.

Additionally, people do not realize how accessible side bar advertising is. Facebook offers people the ability to post a website with a picture and link that will pop up on people's Facebook side bar when logging on and interacting on Facebook. The best way for you to benefit from this is by creating your own website, which is very easily done; you can create a website that highlights who you are as a candidate and the strengths and specialties you can offer a future employer. This is more than a résumé; you can actually post programs you developed, patents you have created, action plans you have composed to address problems in the workplace, etc. This is a branding device that can give a company a clear picture of everything a person can offer beyond the résumé.

## Twitter

Again, here is another website that was initially designed for more of a social interaction than professional business network. Twitter can also be beneficial if you are seriously active in your job search. The more followers the better. When people follow others on Twitter, they grow a loyalty to the people they follow. This allows you to "tweet" your needs for employment and your desire to get back to work. Here you can ask for help. Many people think that such a plea would go unheard, but in actuality many people will respond to your calls for assistance. Even if it is only a job lead or connecting you with another person, everything helps.

## Plaxo

This is similar to LinkedIn and Twitter because it's a blend of both. This site allows you to build a profile with your work history, education, and personal contact information. There are many benefits to the site, but the most significant benefit is its connection to another site, Simply Hired, which allows you to do broad searches of job openings available throughout the country.

YouTube

It's a growing trend for people to use this site as an entertaining outlet. It is now becoming a place where people can post videos, not only asking for a job, but pitching their background to a potential employer. This is commonly referred to as a quick screen interview. You have two to three minutes to state your case. Take some of the most common and strategic questions companies ask of you in an interview in your field and give it a pitch. Tell them what they want to know. You can use this on your website, other social networking sites, or even as a signature when sending your résumé to companies.

Remember, when you are using social networking sites, whether for work and business purposes or not, you have to remember your audience. Is what you are posting on the sites and on your profile what you want everyone to see or hear about you?

Here are some of the most important DO's and DON'Ts of using these sites:

DO's

- Information is power. Make sure you completely set up your profile by filling in all areas and highlighting all the skills and experiences that make your background valuable.
- Advertise or link your social networking sites to each other. Most sites allow you to list other sites you belong to. You can also create a signature on your email and put the links to your sites there as well as on your résumé. Use this as a marketing opportunity to get your name out there.
- Schedule time to use social media sites. You do not want your social media page to go stagnant. Keep it updated. You want people to know about the latest things that are happening in your world, especially as people's needs change along with your own needs.

- Share your accomplishments and successes! This is an opportunity for you to answer interview questions before they are even asked. The most commonly asked questions pertain to your successes in your job and how you have helped your company's bottom line.

- Respond quickly to emails and requests to be "friends" or "contacts." Do not seem uninterested. You do not know what connections that person has or who they know. Just as much as social networking sites can benefit you, they can hurt you. What happens if the person you ignored becomes your future boss?

- Join Groups! Just posting a profile is not going to get you a lot of traffic. You need to get involved in groups and "like" companies and organizations that are going to help you network.

- Use professionalism when writing and interacting on these sites. Make sure you address people properly and make good use of the English language and writing mechanics. Do not use phrases like "yo, what's up" when addressing a manager. Yes, this has happened.

- Give other people references! Remember, when you give other people references then you not only are helping your peers, but they may have someone on their page or their connections that may see you were their boss or colleague and may find interest in your background as well.

- Actively request and accept friend requests. Do not just be a hoarder of requests. Actively seek out new contacts and make requests to expand your network.

- Remember to add value to your profile. Any associations, certifications, specialty training, and knowledge of unique equipment or industry techniques only helps your ability to market yourself.

- Respect the people you are contacting. One thing people forget is that technology has given us unprecedented access to people. This can be to your benefit, but it also can appear to be invasive. Respect a person's profile. Do not riddle them with emails and become a "spammer." If a person does not respond right away. Give them time. Even though we would like to think that everyone keeps up with their social media profile, they don't.

DON'Ts

- Pictures!  Be careful of pictures! One of the biggest mistakes people make is posting illicit or compromising pictures of themselves on their page. Even if you are only using a site for social purposes, think before you post.
- Do not show yourself doing things that many can construe as offensive. Not everyone believes in what you believe. Not everyone supports what you do in your personal time. Future employers look at profiles to know not only who you are, but what you do in your private life. This is commonly an area of discrimination.
- Spell-Check!  Email, Internet Pages, Posts, and Social Sites have become a very relaxed way to communicate. The problem is that commonly people forget to use proper English (spelling and grammar) when communicating on these sites. This includes not using impersonal slang and phrases (yeah, gotcha, what's up, yo, dude, etc.). Pretend you are talking to your boss, not your best friend. Remember that your posts can be seen, e-mails can be forwarded, and pictures can be tagged!
- Avoid comments that can be viewed as discriminatory, racists, ageist, sexist, or any other anti-anything.
- Be careful on the types of jokes you use. Just like discriminatory comments, people can be offended by what you say. Say things you would be comfortable saying in your place of work, not at the bar on your third glass of beer.

- Do not bad mouth your present or previous employers! Remember that these sites are like an interview. This is your opportunity for them to get a picture of who you are and what you represent.

- Do not publicly post that you are looking for a job unless your current employer knows you are looking. Many states are known as right-to-work states. This means that employers can lay you off with no cause. You do not want to be dismissed simply because you are looking for other opportunities.

- Do not become a spammer! Be courteous. You do not want to overuse and commercialize your interaction with people. The key is to make it somewhat personalized when pursuing a contact or a company to engage in. Do not make it a general tactic that you use with everyone. No canned emails!

- Often times you will feel rejected. People will not email you back. Someone may reject your invitation to become connected. Do not take offense to this. Just move on. Focus on the positive, not the negative.

- Keep your medical- and health-related issues to yourself. Be careful how much you disclose. Even publicizing the fact that you smoke can damage your image. There are many companies that drive initiatives to hire non-smokers.

- Do not post personal pictures of yourself if you do not think it will benefit you in your search. The picture you do post should be professional and best represent you as an individual. No glamour shots! Professional but subtle.

- Companies do log internet use! Do not think that your internet use is a secret when you are using it at work.

Social Networking is not going away, it is only going to get more extensive and more widely used. Do not be scared of engagement. If you lack computer skills or need help navigating these sites, there are plenty of free community classes and online tutorials to help you navigate these sites. Unfortunately, I know of many people who are not very computer savvy and would find these sites overwhelming and almost impossible to understand. But with advancements in technology comes the need to become proficient with new technologies.

Remember that when you are networking on these sites, it is all about branding yourself. Only say, do, post, and communicate what you want people to judge you by. Everyone is watching.

Tim has no idea where to begin. Although he has been working for over 25 years, he is not the most computer savvy person. He has never been on a social networking site, let alone built a profile on one. Tim decides it probably would be a good idea to go to a local community college and take a class on working with the internet. Part of the class training is focused on how to sign up and navigate job boards and social networking sites and how to build profiles. He knows it is important for him to get his name out there.

Marketing is Samantha's life! So for her, being on social networking sites and being involved in group discussions and blogs is a necessity. Because she already is actively involved in the social networking arena, she expands her involvement by getting on the jobs sections of the different sites to locate possible positions that she can apply for. She also starts to contact some of her connections in LinkedIn to see if they can forward her information to other connections that they have to help her market her background to different companies.

George has become increasingly frustrated with his job search. But he knows he needs to do whatever he can to find a position for himself and his family. He starts to blog about his skills and experience on some of the social networking sites. He also joins groups and engages with current group members on his background and how he feels he can possibly help their companies. He knows how difficult his job search will be, so he has to do everything possible to make it successful.

Pete has vast experience in building profiles on various social sites. The problem is he has only used them for his personal/social life and not his professional life. Pictures of him drinking, partying, and having a good time litter his profile pages. He first decides he needs to clean up his profile and make it attractive to companies. Once he does that he will start using his connections and friends to network and try to find possible opportunities. A lot of the job boards actually link company jobs to profiles and so many of the jobs get automatically posted on these boards as well.

# HANDLING INTERVIEW QUESTIONS

The key to any successful phone interview or face-to-face interview is in how you present yourself and answer questions asked of you. The focus that you should keep when answering questions is how you would bring value to the organization. Every question you respond to should consist of ways you can add value to the company.

There are two major areas of questions you have to be prepared for. There are open-ended questions that are a subjective evaluation of who you are and what you bring to the company. Then there are behavioral questions that truly dig into your overall ability to create value to the organization.

Open-ended questions

These are questions that ask for general information about you. They can be very simple questions, but could have incredibly significant effects on your job search. Let's look at some of these questions and how you should respond or handle such questions.

**Tell me about yourself.**

- This is a question that most people hope for because it gives you the opportunity to disclose any information about yourself. But the dangers of this question are that people do not pay attention to how much they are saying and for how long they are talking. Think about the job description, the company philosophies and vision, and focus a two or three minute response on ways that you can align yourself with the company.

**Are you a team player?**

- The easy answer for everyone is "yes." Do you really think that anyone would say they are not a team player? This question is a chance to discuss how you have engaged in team activities with prior organizations and enjoyed collaborating with a diverse group of people. Talk about using positive ideas from different people to come to a solution to a problem. Minimize the use of the word "I."

**What would be one of your greatest weaknesses?**

- First – everyone has weaknesses. Do not ever say, "I don't have any weaknesses." Come prepared to answer this question. The key to the weakness question is to take a weakness and turn it into a potential strength. Take one of my weaknesses for an example— I like to beat a dead horse, which is to say I do not give up very easily. This is a weakness because sometimes you have to be willing to let go and move forward. Because some problems cannot be solved, I'm wasting time when I continue working for a solution. But people that beat a dead horse really tend to think outside the box and look at things from different angles. They are not stuck on a single solution. So even though they may take a longer time to solve a problem, they certainly address it in many more ways than others. They ultimately find solutions for problems more than people who try one solution and then give up.

**What qualities are you looking for in a manager?**

- Be very careful with this question. There are really few qualities that you can always expect in a manager. Focus on things that most managers are going to possess: leadership, vision, profit-focused methods, and employee development training programs. Try to avoid things you like and do not like in managers because it is a gamble on what the interviewer feels about managers' qualities.

**Give me an example of when you disagreed with a boss or coworker, and how did you resolve it?**

- Again, you should always have an answer ready for this question. Everyone disagrees with bosses or co-workers sometime during his or her career. The most effective responses to this question will illustrate your desire to understand the other person's perspective. By showing that you are open to understanding why the other person thinks the way they do, you show that you are team-oriented and willing to accept change.

**Why should I hire you?**

- Avoid generalities and certainly don't say, "Because I'm definitely the one for the job." This is a good opportunity to talk about some of your strengths and skills that you know are highly applicable to the job, especially to highlight those skills that will brand you as the best candidate. Remember to fully answer the question but keep your responses brief

**If you were to change anything in your current or most recent job, what would it be and why?**

- Again be careful not to be too narrowly focused. Use general things that people often times desire in most opportunities. Talk about wanting someone that can mentor you to help you learn and grow as you contribute to the company's growth. Talk about strong management support in decisions that you make in your job. Discuss things that you know every company needs in order for the company to succeed.

**Why were you fired?**

- The best thing you can do here is be brief and vague. The most common response and best response is along the lines of, "Over the years I have had several successful relationships with the companies and managers I have worked for. My most recent manager and I just agreed that our goals and overall expectations on where we would like this position to go (or how to handle problems within the environment) were not corresponding." I understand there are a lot more circumstances where this answer would not apply. Also, remind the interviewer of the fact you were never fired before, and you have a lot of great references that will support your abilities within their environment. Also try to come prepared with a reference from a manager at the company you were fired from that will counter any concerns.

### How would you describe yourself?

- Focus on teams and working in a collaborative environment. Things you should talk about is seeing others opinions to help make cohesive decisions and working together in teams to address problems. Talk about being highly efficient, dedicated, and always expending all your energy to get the job done.

### How do you pace your day-to-day work?

- I tend to work at a steady pace but always tend to finish work before the scheduled time needed for it to be completed. I like to beat the expected time frame of the company to allow time to go back and review the work or decision, and to find ways I might perfect it in the future.

### How do you handle stress?

- First make sure you emphasize that you do not allow stress to take over your life and distract you from your goals. The best way to manage stress for you is to balance it with your work and find ways to prioritize. Prioritizing in a stressful situation or environment allows you to find solutions faster and address the most urgent needs.

**What is your biggest motivation when you are at work?**

- Feeling accomplished and making an impact in the organization will make the company feel you are not merely looking out for yourself but that you consider the company's best interest. Focus your motivation on what benefits both parties, rather than being strictly self-interested.

**What would you say are some of people's top criticisms of who you are?**

- This is an easy question, but often times answered poorly. The key is to not give an answer. The best way to answer this is to explain to the interviewer that any feedback or advice that a person gives you is information to help you grow personally and professionally, therefore it really is not criticism but a tool promoting improvement.

**Do you prefer to be involved in teams or handle things on your own?**

- Again, do not take a stance. There is no reason why you cannot be happy in both environments. Explain to the interviewer that depending on the circumstances and situation, working in teams is more beneficial, and in other situations working as a support agent or individual will benefit the company more.

**Why do you want this job?**

- Focus not only on the opportunity but also on the company. Do not just make it about a job. Make sure you focus your answer on how you feel this job can help you grow as an individual, and how it can be a job in which you can help grow the organization. You should also express how you feel this job at the company would allow you to succeed because of the history of the company supporting its employees.

## What do you know about our company, our brands?

- This is why you need to do research before the interview. Be prepared to answer this question. It can come in many avenues and in many forms. You need to be able to talk about the company's history, the future of the company, and make sure you are able to identify brands, services, or programs that are representative of the company and not its competitors.

## What types of challenges would you like to have in your new role?

- It is impossible for you to tell what challenges are going to occur in the job you are about to attain. The best way to answer this question is to focus on your interest to use your skills, experiences, and your talents to impact the company. Simply put, you do not want to be underutilized. Explain to the interviewer that you want them to utilize your talents to maximize your potential.

## What are you goals for the next 2, 5, and 10 years?

- Focus on general expectations; do not be narrow-minded in your response. Talk about being a top contributor and performer in the company. Talk about being able to constantly make an impact and continuously grow within the company so you can help the company grow. Explain to the interviewer that you trust the company that you are working for will create a plan to help further develop you within the organization and make you a more important asset to the success of the company.

**How do you feel if I tell you that I do not feel you are the most qualified for this job?**

- Do not take no as an answer. Be confident. Explain to the company that you truly believe that your achievements and skills can be utilized in many facets within the organization to help the organization succeed. That it is not always the most qualified person that will be the most successful person in the role. Sometimes it is all about a person's drive and passion that makes him or her successful.

**Aren't you a bit overqualified to do this role? Why would this position interest you?**

- During the recent recession this has become a tremendous issue and concern of many companies. Many of the unemployed have taken steps back in their careers in order to be employed. The best way to react to this question is to acknowledge the job market and emphasize that you have come to the conclusion that you believe if you get with the right company and prove yourself through performance, that, in time, you will be able to continue to grow your career and get back to and exceed where you were before.

**Why have you been out of work for so long?**

- Don't make excuses. The best thing to tell an employer is that you are not going to just take a job. You are looking for a company that you truly believe you can be successful in and plan on taking a position with a company to be with them long-term. Emphasize that you are a loyal employee, and that cannot change just because you are unemployed. You have to believe that the companies you are going to work for believe you can be successful.

**If you are able to go back and make any changes in how you lived your life, what would they be and why?**

- The best response for this question is to take ownership for your choices in life. You can learn from every choice you make, especially the wrong choices. Emphasize that although you accept the fact that some of your decisions in the past may not have been the best decision possible, you learned from those decisions and how to make them better.

**Why are you looking to leave your current employer?**

- The number one thing to remember is ALWAYS turn this into a positive by saying what you are "looking for in your future employer" rather than talking about what your current company is lacking. For example, if your current company has no program for advancement, then say, "I am looking for a company of which I can be a part of their long-term growth and succeed in my abilities to continue to grow my career." Another example would be if you have a boss that doesn't help you develop or work on your areas of development. You might say, "I would like to work for a company that values employee development and helps its employees develop areas of opportunities within their abilities so that they can apply these strengths to future leadership within the company." The last thing you want to do is talk negatively about your employer by saying the company lacks growth opportunities, or that your boss does not do anything to help you develop.

Other sample questions that get asked in interviews:

- How would you differentiate a good job from an excellent job?
- Why are you better than all the other candidates that we are interviewing?
- How would you describe your ideal boss?
- What rewards would you like to gain from your job?
- What do you know about our company, and why do you feel it would be the best place for you to work?
- How long would it take for you to start to make an impact within our company?
- What do you think is the biggest challenge in your job search?
- If your spouse does not plan to move with you to your new job location, what would motivate you to stay with us long-term?
- Have you ever had to terminate someone and how did it go?
- What do you not like about your most recent position?
- When you walk into a room, do you approach people and introduce yourself or do you wait for them to approach you?
- How do you go about building a team?
- If I were to talk to your coworkers or subordinates, what would they say about you?
- What describes success to you?
- How have you helped your past employers increase profitability, reduce cost or waste, or increase sales?

Behavioral Questions

The other type of interview questions commonly used in interviewing is Behavioral Questions. These types of questions are becoming more and more common in the interview process and probably are emphasized more than any other types of questions that a company can ask you.

STAR (Situation, Task, Action, and Results) is an acronym that best outlines the purpose and expectations of these types of questions:

- Situation – This describes the problem or situation you are trying to address and the problem you are trying to solve
- Task - What is the ultimate goal or end result that you are trying to accomplish?
- Action – What actions did you take to address the problem and reach the ideal goal or result?
- Results – What are the positive end results of your approach?

The use of the STAR method has become a growing trend because it allows a company to evaluate your capabilities of dealing with problems within a work environment and finding solutions to drive the changes for success. It is very important to focus on specific experiences you have been involved in. The biggest mistake that people make when answering these types of questions is the use of hypothetical examples. Be prepared to use real life examples!

The best way to prepare for behavioral questions and the STAR method is to recall as many problems and actions you have taken in the past to drive success. Be prepared to give descriptions, brief but specific, that will best allow the interviewer to understand what type of problem you were dealing with and how you drove a better result. Make sure the outcome of how you addressed the problem was a positive one. Confessing a failure to bring about a positive result will only damage the interviewer's image of you.

Understanding the Score Card System – General Competencies

Remember that every interviewer is going to be evaluating you based on a scorecard and many different behaviors during the interview process. It is very important to remember that you are not only rated on your answers, but on how you come across during the interview.

Here are some examples of things you may be evaluated for:

- Oral and Written Communication
- Problem Solving
- Interpersonal Skills
- Reaction Time to Questions
- Nature of Responses
- Verbalization and Articulation of Answers
- Adaptability
- Attitude
- Teamwork
- Leadership
- Listening
- Presentation Skills
- Confidence
- Initiative
- Ability to take Risks
- Establishing Rapport
- Stress Management
- Flexibility
- Work Ethic
- Excitement and Energy

## Goal of Behavioral Interviews

The ultimate goal of a Behavioral-based Interview is for you to discuss how you have approached situations in the past and what results you achieved through your actions. The questions used in the interview process are typically standardized for each company and individual position. By making the questions standardized it creates consistency and cohesiveness when scoring the interviews. With each question, the interviewee is scored on how he or she describes the situation, discusses the task established, details what actions are taken to address the situation, and reports the end results. The score card measures a candidate's proficiency in many of the areas listed above as well as additional areas determined by the company.

Most companies that use these types of interviews are also looking for measurable results in a candidate's ability to impact an organization. Companies are not only looking for your style of leadership or handling of the situation, but whether you are able to drive measurable results that will affect the bottom line. More information on types of measurable results is discussed in later chapters.

The interviewer is not only trying to measure you in many areas and work required for the job, but they are also trying to differentiate candidates that make good and bad decisions. So be cognizant to only use examples that were clearly good leadership and strategic decisions leading to positive results for the company.

No candidate has every skill that a position requires. Companies are going to determine which skills and experiences are trainable and which skills are not. Ask questions and pay attention to the types of questions that are being asked and what they are focusing on; this will help you better understand what skills are required for candidates versus what the company believes it can teach new hires.

Preparing for Behavioral Interviews

It is very important to prepare for a Behavioral Interview. If you are not sure about what type of interview will be conducted, you can either ask the company concerning types of questions and format the interview will be in or you can assume that some of the interviews will be behavioral-based and prepare for them. Behavioral interviews are definitely the trend and will likely occur during the hiring process.

Make sure you are familiar with the position and the requirements for the position. Gain as much information as possible on the needs of the role so you can use examples during the interview that will highlight your strengths in these areas. It is better to use examples that directly correlate to the position and will impact the role, instead of examples that are irrelevant.

Once you have familiarized yourself with the position, think of stories and examples of situations that have occurred in your personal work experience that relate to the role. Be prepared to draw from these examples in order to reflect on your ability to handle the needs and responsibilities of the role. The situations and examples that you likely will offer are going to be work related, though personal situations that can be related to the role can also be used.

Remember the STAR method when answering each question/situation. Each question will involve you to break down the situation/task that you are addressing, report on what types of actions you took to address them, and describe what results were driven from these actions. This method is designed to help the interviewer understand how you handle particular situations and ultimately how you will drive future performance within their company. This gives the interviewer a way to predict your future performance.

Lastly, make sure that you use recent situations that have occurred in the last 3-5 years. I realize that you may have 20 years of experience and may have accomplished a lot in your career, but try to cite examples and situations that are more recent. If you are unable to think of an example that is recent on a particular question, you can always fall back on using an older example. Companies want to know that you have continued to address situations and grow in your career by doing so.

If the interviewer asks you questions that you find difficult to answer and you are having a problem thinking of an example, you have two options: first, you can ask the interviewer if you can come back to that question later in the interview. By doing this you are giving yourself some time to think of an example that will work well with the question. Second, explain to the interviewer that you cannot think of an example that exactly fits the question, but you can give them an example that is similar and in close alignment with the point of the question.

<u>Types of Responses</u>

There are two good types of responses to behavior questions. There are positive situations with positive results, and negative situations with positive results. The importance of these two distinct types of responses is that companies not only want to know you can help address problems within the organization, but also that you can recognize ways to improve situations or environments that are working well but still have the ability to grow and improve. This touches on the concept that you can always find ways to make improvements. Nothing and no one is ever perfect.

The most important thing to consider when responding to behavioral questions is for your response to be positive. Make sure that regardless whether the situation started positively or negatively that you communicate that the end result you brought about was a positive gain overall.

Use numbers when giving examples of your results so the company can quantify your success or accomplishment. Be consistent with your numbers to avoid the appearance of lying. You don't need to give them all the details of the situation; leave them room to ask questions. Paint for them a clear picture of the situation, the actions taken, and the results driven.

I often use an analogy to describe the importance of clarity in your examples. Imagine walking into an art gallery and on one side of the wall you see a Van Gogh, and on the other side of the gallery you see a Picasso. When you look at the Van Gogh, you clearly perceive what object or detail the painter was painting. You may not necessarily understand the overall meaning intended by the painter, but you generally can see a clear picture.

It is not the same with a Picasso. Take a look at the Picasso and the first question you ask yourself is, "What in the world is this?" Most Picasso paintings are very hard to interpret and generally the picture is very unclear. When you are answering questions in an interview, make sure to paint a Van Gogh, not a Picasso.

Be prepared to discuss with the interviewer the reason that you took the action you took. Interviewers often times want to understand your thought process on why you decided to approach the situation the way you did. They are not necessarily questioning your decision, but trying to understand your decision-making process. Make sure you stay relaxed and simply explain the reasoning of your decision. Most importantly, be confident. Do not allow the interviewer to make you question your decision. An interviewer wants someone who is going to stand by his or her decisions.

Things to Remember when Answering Behavior Questions
- Remember to use the STAR Method
- Keep your answers directed to the question asked; do not stray to a different topic or situation.
- Keep responses short. Limit your answers to two to three minutes. Do not allow yourself to ramble or you will lose the interest of the interviewer.
- Try to use as many specifics in your example, including numbers, to emphasize the measured results you were able to drive with your actions.
- If you are unsure of what the interviewer is looking for in the question, do not be afraid to ask clarifying questions.
- Give yourself a second to think of the best example before answering the question. The worst thing you can do is start talking about a situation only to realize it is not relevant to the question.
- Focus on your own actions in addressing the question. Do not involve other people's actions because it could cloud the success of how your actions impacted the results.
- Make sure not to lie! Often companies will ask you the same question multiple times in different forms during different parts of your interview process to make sure there is consistency among your answers.

- Focus on your strengths, not your weaknesses. However, do not cite too many strengths in any single response. Your strengths will be evident by the end of the interview and hiring processes.
- Make sure that you focus on the areas of your experience that are going to be critical to the success of the job.

Here are some examples of types of Behavioral Questions. Try to use quantifiable (numerical) examples that can measure performance:

- **Describe a situation where you had to solve a difficult problem. What caused the problem, and how did you go about finding a solution?** The best type of response would be to change the negative to a positive. In this case they are clearly looking for a well-defined problem (or negative issue) within the workplace and how you went about turning it into a positive result. Make sure to not speak negatively about peers or other employees within the company when describing the situation unless the problem was specifically an employee-related developmental problem.

- **Describe to me a time you made a quick decision that ultimately created a positive return?** This situation can be where you created or developed something in order to improve an existing system or program, or took a problem and found a solution.

- **Think about a time when you are were having issues dealing with a coworker or a subordinate and how did you handle the situation?** In this case it's obvious that you have to speak to negative terms on why there was an issue. The most important thing to remember is to avoid any situations where you were the problem or might be perceived to have been the problem. Use a clear example where the specific employee was not responsive to your coaching or leadership.

- **Tell me about a time when you had to address a problem on your own without the use of any support or other employees, and how did you accomplish it?** Companies not only need to know that you can work in a team-based environment and work well with others, but they also need to know that you can be self-sufficient on dealing with day-to-day tasks on your own when needed.

- **Describe a time when you did not want to handle a situation or task and you were able to delegate it to another individual.** This question definitely can be answered with a situational-based response. Be careful to describe the situation or task, how you delegated it to another person, and how that person succeeded effectively.

- **Describe a time when you had to make a decision that was not popular among your team or department.** Questions like this can be fairly general in scope. So do not be afraid to draw on any type of situation, even potential situations from a personal spectrum.

- **Describe a time when you set a goal and were unable to accomplish it.** In this case the obvious result would seem negative, but you can always use this situation as a learning experience and then reflect on how it made you better or stronger for future situations. Your response to this question could strategically segue into a more positive example. You can describe how after this failure you used what you learned to create a positive result in a subsequent situation.

- **Tell me about a time when you had a major obstacle you had to overcome and how you overcame it.** Again, this can be fairly general in scope. But this is definitely an opportunity to use numbers and measurable results. Try to find a situation where you had a goal, met an obstacle, discovered a way around the obstacle, and experienced a positive result from your efforts. Make sure to give details concerning the obstacle, how you side-stepped it, and the positive results that followed.

- **Describe a time where you had to convince someone who did not agree with how you wanted to handle a problem to ultimately agree to handle it your way.** This not only illustrates your ability to be persuasive, but ultimately shows how persuading you are able to persuade a colleague to drive a positive, measurable impact to the organization's performance.

- **Tell me of a time that you had to talk to your supervisor on how he or she handled a problem and how it impacted your work environment.** In this case you are looking for a situation where you were confronting an individual and how you went about doing this. In what type of environment and circumstances did you handle this conversation, how did you approach explaining the issue, and how did you drive a positive response that created a learning experience for everyone involved.

- **Tell me about a situation where you recognized a potential problem before it occurred and what preventative steps you took to keep it from becoming an actual problem.** This questions offers another great opportunity to talk about how you have saved a company money or ways to prevent cost of down-time or financial burdens on a company had the problem actually occurred.

- **Tell me about a time when you were forced to partner with another person to solve a problem, and he/she did not particularly care for you.** This is another great way to show how you can use the art of persuasiveness and the best practices approach in handling a person that you have had challenges with in the past. This could involve being on a team that you did not necessarily have the lead on, but you helped drive the results while working with this individual.

- **Describe an occurrence where you were asked to address a problem that was not necessarily your responsibility, or where you were not skilled in the area of interest.** In this example you can describe how you used other people help solve the problem. A great example would be drawing on the strengths of other individuals, especially in an area where you lack experience.

- **Discuss a situation where you decided to go against a company policy because you felt it would hinder your ability to solve a problem, and how you ultimately justified your decision.** Be careful not to discuss situations that ended up causing you to be terminated or relieved of your position. Generally, you want to focus on a situation where even though you did not follow company policies you were still rewarded because you are were able to solve the problem and potentially save the company money.

- **Everyone has strengths; tell me about your greatest weakness. Use this opportunity to take a weakness and turn it into a positive.** The best way would be to talk about even though you are weak in a certain area you were able to overcome this weakness to still confront and resolve a problem that you were addressing.

- **Describe a situation where you knew that when you resolved a problem it would make another individual look bad and how you handled it.** This is an excellent opportunity to talk about not only that by taking action you drove a positive result, but it is also an opportunity to show how create a positive result and learning experience while resolving conflicts.

Obviously there are countless questions and scenarios you might experience during an interview. The types of questions and styles of questioning remind you that you need to be prepared for any possible scenario that is put in front of you. Remember that if a question is posed to you, and you cannot think of an immediate response, it is perfectly reasonable and professional to ask if you can come back to the question. However, use this option sparingly.

Creating Value

The most important thing to remember when answering questions is to focus on creating value in the mind of the interviewer. Companies ultimately determine the need for an employee based on how the candidate will impact the company's successful in the long-term. It is important to envision yourself in the organization and remember to answer in a way that communicates a purpose and value to being a part of the team.

If a company perceives the value in you being a part of its organization, they know you will help drive the business forward. The goal of any business is to grow long-term and meet the company's long-term goals, strategy, and vision. If you are able to evidence the value of you being with the company to meet these needs, you are heading in the right direction.

Over the years, Tim has interviewed and hired many manufacturing hourlies and management personnel. He understands the needs of using clear, tangible, detailed examples when talking about the success he has brought to the companies he has worked for. The biggest technique he has to practice is to not be negative about his lack of degree and focus his attention on highlighting his lean manufacturing experience and how he can drive profits within an organization. He has many examples of how he improved productivity, retention, and waste within his departments and the cost savings it has brought to his employers.

Samantha is happy in her current job, but because she doesn't feel fulfilled in her job and wants to get into a position that is more branding-focused. She knows that her responses to the interviewers' questions should be focused on the branding aspect of her background. If asked why she wants to leave her current employer, her responses will center on her desire to refocus her career to a branding emphasis. She will definitely make clear her satisfaction with her current employer and that her job search is motivated by her desire to get into a more branding-focused position. When citing examples of her achievements and strengths, she is going to focus all her efforts on the work she has done with branding.

George has been in the personal consumer finance investment business for years and is trying to get into the corporate finance investment world. He knows the most effective tactic in his interviews will be to use examples of how he has taken certain situations and created positive results. He is going to use the STAR method when answering the questions focused on the customer/client situations, the clients' need to see results, the actions taken to affect the best results, and ultimately the results that followed. He knows that by showing positive financial gains for his personal consumers, a company will recognize the opportunity of him investing for them.

As a new college graduate with no experience, Pete is going to focus on many different types of situations in his life where he has driven positive change, led and managed people, and created an impact. He is going to use his involvement in several elected positions in college and high school, along with a summer internship, in addition to the work experience he gained during college. He knows that companies value a candidate's experiences; he has a lot of experiences in these environments that will prove to be valuable.

# PREPARING FOR A PHONE INTERVIEW

If you ask me what my least favorite part of the interview process is, my opinion will never change—it is the phone interview! The phone interview is your first opportunity to keep the interest of the company. Unfortunately, this is also an opportunity for you to lose the company's interest. It's also one of the most impersonal ways of getting to know someone. So it is very important to treat the phone interview as the most critical aspect of the process because it can make or break your opportunity moving forward.

Remember you are always interviewing. Just because a manager, recruiter, or contact is not calling your conversation a phone interview, you are always being interviewed. Do not forget this; one of the easiest ways for people to lose the opportunity is by becoming too relaxed and thinking that it's just a conversation. Later in this chapter we will discuss the dos and don'ts of phone interviews.

Types of Phone Interviews

There are many types of phone interviews that you need to prepare for:

- Direct-Hire:  These are conversations that you have with the hiring authority, the person that you would actually be working for. This is probably the most critical conversation because they are the ultimate decision-maker. This is usually not the first conversation you have with a company, but it can be a critical turning point in your pursuit of the position.

- Indirect-Hire:  Often called "gate-keepers," these are the people who the hiring manager has as pre-screeners. Often human resources or internal corporate recruiting are given a list of qualifications and questions that the hiring manager is looking to know before deciding to move forward with you as a candidate.

- Third Party: Recruiters are a screening mechanism for companies so that they do not have to deal directly with the barrage of résumés that come in on a daily basis. Recruiters, however, cannot only be a gate-keeper for the company; they could also be your best cheerleader. They have insights into the company.

- Referrals: When you network, you often ask people to represent you to someone they know. Remember, these people are putting their names on the line by presenting you and your credentials to their contact. How this person views you will be a huge part of how they decide to promote you as a candidate.

- Pre-Screening Questionnaires: Due to companies' increasing dependence on the internet for finding qualified candidates, many companies and recruiters are utilizing online pre-screening questionnaires and tests to weed out candidates. Take pre-screen questionnaires just as seriously, if not more, than the actual phone screen itself. People not only judge you by the information you present through a pre-screening questionnaire, but by how you present this information; spelling, grammar, and overall organization of your presentation will influence the hiring committee.

- Company Representatives: In your networking efforts, you will meet people who work for the company and know of openings but who are not the direct hiring manager. Similar to those who refer you; those you meet through networking may not know you very well. This means their initial impressions of you will be critical.

Your primary objective during the phone interview is to gain the confidence and support of the person on the other end. This person is your initial advocate with the company and can help you move forward in the job process. You want the person convinced that they like you and can't see anything that would concern them regarding your ability to do the job.

The decision to hire someone is typically based on five core factors:
- Overall Attitude and Professional Poise
- Clear and Concise Presentation and Communication Skills
- Level of Experience and Skill Set
- Education and Certifications Achieved
- Transferable Industry and Technical Capabilities

Turn the phone interview into a win-win for both parties. It is important to move forward in the process, but it is also important to have an advocate. The last thing you want is the person on the other end of the phone to perceive you as just another candidate. Make an impression. The interviewer's time is valuable, so respect that person's time. This will lead them to respect and appreciate you more.

Purpose of a Phone Interview

What is important to remember when doing a phone interview is to create value to the company and in the mind of the interviewer. I often use the following example:

Imagine walking on to a used car lot and looking over several cars. You find the car that you've always wanted as the salesperson walks up to you to discuss the vehicle and its price. The salesperson wants $40,000 for the car, yet all the books and websites you have researched show the value of the car to be lower. The salesperson has to then create a value to you. He has to somehow convince you there are things about this particular car that you will not find with any other car of its kind. Whether it is selling you on the unique body kit, the high performance modified engine, the limited edition of the year/make/model, or the special color, the salesperson has to create a value to you on why you would pay more for this car versus a comparable car.

View all your conversations during the interview process as opportunities to increase your value in the minds of the hiring committee members. They need to feel that by bringing you on board they are going to see a monetary gains and profitable effects.

Some examples of things that create value:

- Demonstrated successes in similar roles where you have driven profitable increase in volume or sales, or unique solutions to company problems.
- Special training and skills limited to people in your field, but seen as exclusive or highly desired.
- Implementation of programs and initiatives that directly affect the bottom line.
- Ability to communicate in various languages.
- Knowledge of a unique process, system, or product that is competitor-specific or industry-common.
- Experience in growing employees beyond the roles or positions they were originally hired for.

Know Company Demands

Know the demands of the companies in your field of business. What are the most common challenges and problems that companies face? Consider your role to help the company meet, exceed, and grow beyond those challenges.

When you identify the needs companies typically have in the industry or type of work you are targeting, it will help you focus your interview. This will also keep you from volunteering information that could detract the employer from wanting to hire you.

## Setting up the Call

When provided the opportunity to pre-schedule a phone interview, make sure you pick a date and time that will allow you the least amount of distractions and minimize background noise. Try to do the phone interview on a dedicated landline versus a cellular phone. Cellular technology has improved our day-to-day communication, but it is hardly reliable for a phone interview. Even though it may appear the interviewer can hear you, they may not, and they might not tell you they cannot.

When scheduling a phone interview, make sure you prepare prior to the call. Have notes in front of you to remind you of discussion points, including your résumé. Make sure you can, with detail, supplement every topic and entry with personal experiences and rehearsed responses to the commonly asked questions. One of the benefits of a phone interview versus a face-to-face interview is your ability to cheat! You can have any information in front of you to help guide you in the conversation. Also, do yourself a favor by blocking out 15-30 minutes prior to the call to allow yourself sufficient time to reach the location where you will receive the call. Do not wait till the last minute. If you are not available when the phone rings, your opportunity with the company could be lost.

## Basics to Remember

Do not forget the common sense basics to a phone interview:

- Shut up and Listen! You are being interviewed; you are not the interviewer. You cannot be listening if you are talking. Also, if you start responding to an interviewer's question before he or she finishes the question, it's clear you weren't listening. In order to truly listen, you have to hear everything they are saying and then think about how you will respond. You might hear the interviewer say, "Give me an example of your biggest accomplishment," as you cut them off and start talking. But you may have missed the rest of the question: "Give me an example of your biggest accomplishment when you were heading a committee or a team." Can you see how not listening could hurt your chances and make you seem arrogant and impatient?

- Project your voice and enunciate your words clearly and concisely. It does not do any good for you or them if the interviewer cannot hear or understand what you are saying. Do not eat, chew gum, or put any other objects in your mouth. Do not cup your palm around your face. Keep any distraction, visual, auditory, or tactile, from interfering with the call. Remember to slow down when you speak. The interviewer is likely taking notes and you do not want them to miss anything.

- Sound passionate and excited about the opportunity. Do you want the job or not? How you project your voice on the phone can be the first signs of your enthusiasm for the company or the role.

- Do not get too informal or personal. Throughout the entire interview process you have to remember you are being interviewed. Do not go into your life story, and do not get into personal aspects of your life. There will be many times where you will feel comfortable with the interviewer and it may seem very easy to slip into this comfort zone. Be on guard. I'm not saying you cannot talk about personal likes and dislikes, but just remember the person on the other end may be offended or have a different opinion. Try to stay in neutral territory, and if you do talk personal, let them initiate that type of conversation.

- Remember to speak in a professional tone and do not use slang or phrases that are used in a relaxed, personal setting. Starting a conversation with, "What up John?" is not going to land you the job.

- Do not talk money, benefits, or salary! You will be tempted toward this topic. We will discuss this more in subsequent chapters.

- Because you cannot see the other person, remember to take short pauses to make sure the person on the other side does not want to interject or ask for clarification.

- Do not be selfish during the phone interview. Again, remember that this is an opportunity for them to interview you. You, of course, will be able to interview them later. The principal purpose of the conversation is for the company to better understand your employment history and experiences you have obtained during your career.

- Focus on the questions asked. A very common mistake is to take a question as an invitation to "sell your background." If the interviewer asks you about your biggest accomplishment, then give them just that – your biggest accomplishment. Do not divert the conversation tangentially toward topics that show your strengths. You're your strengths while answering the interviewer's particular question. What they ask is what they want to know. Stay focused. Most companies have a list of questions to help them learn or confirm pertinent details within the constraints of a phone interview. If you waste time answering questions they don't ask, you risk running out of time and not providing the company with the information most important to them.

- Do not be long-winded and don't babble. This complements the previous bullet. You want your words to be economical and focused. The last thing the interviewer wants is to listen to you talk for 30 minutes.

- Avoid discriminatory remarks, especially because you don't know the interviewer's race, age, religious affiliation, sexual orientation, etc. Using expletives or remarks that can be taken as discriminatory is a cause for an immediate end to a conversation.
- Do not disclose your age. I don't care that you believe that this is the reason you lost the last three job interviews. Telling a company or a recruiter your age upfront so you don't waste anyone's time is evident that you lack confidence in your abilities to learn and grow in any environment.

These are many of the basic things you need to keep in mind during your phone screen. Many of these seem fairly basic and common sense. Believe it or not, if I mentioned it, it has happened. This is why it is important to constantly remind yourself of interview etiquette when on that call.

Dissect the Job Description

Dissect the job description prior to the call. Take each requirement and objective of the job and write down experiences in your background that illustrate how you might meet the needs of the interviewing company. Also be prepared to have key points at hand when doing the phone interview itself, especially if the interview questions are open ended.

Examples of key points:
- What type of experience do they want?
- Are they asking for any specific technical skills or computer/systems knowledge?
- Does this position require more people management or project / systems management?
- Are there any skills they list as a plus that you possess?

- Does the company look for a degree? Bachelors? Masters? Are they looking for a specific major?
- What skills does the job description focus on?

## Research the Company

Do research on the company before the phone call. This will enable you to be prepared with questions that will help you better understand the company and its needs. This will also dictate the way you want to respond too many of the questions, or questions you may want to ask.

## Understanding the Content of a Phone Interview

Remember, this could be the most important call during the entire process. This is the call that will allow you either to move forward or lose the opportunity altogether. This is also a great opportunity to become more informed and prepare for the face-to-face interview.

Most companies just take notes to standard questions they are prepared to ask, however many companies have shifted to a scorecard system in interviews and phone interviewers. The scorecard system allows the interviewer to rate a person on a scale from 1 to 5 on skills that will be important to the position. Generally, most hiring managers have a set number of questions that they are looking to complete by the end of the conversation. They add up all the numbers on the scorecard at the end and it gives them a form of evaluation of your strength for the position.

Common areas evaluated in scorecard interviews are:

### Personal Skills
- Listening skills
- Leadership
- Able to adapt to different environments
- Drive, passion, and overall energy
- Ability to coach employees

- Interpersonal skills
- Communication (strong use of the English Language)
- Understanding and knowledge of the company
- Analytical skills
- Willingness to do what it takes to get the job done
- Confidence
- Goal-driven

Technical Capabilities
- Technical or Systems Knowledge
- Lean or Continuous Improvement
- Use of Automated Technology or Systems
- Years of Technical Skills for the Job
- Working with Vendors / Outside Resources

Listen for phrases or comments that the interviewer makes with regards to the company's needs and the position.
- We need someone who...
- This person has to be able to...
- What is most important is...
- We would like to see...
- My goal in hiring this person is...
- The ideal person will...

Be prepared for questions that may be very direct. Never feel insulted or embarrassed. Do not allow a question to fluster you or make you feel that it is a personal attack. Use a question as an opportunity to explain who you are and what you can bring to the table.

The following are common questions that could appear as personal attacks, but really are just concerns that need clarification:

- It appears you have had a lot of jobs over the last 10 years; can you help me understand the reason for these changes?
- Based on your application and résumé, it does not seem you really have ever grown or developed in your career. What have you done to develop yourself and further grow the companies you have been with?
- You seem very confident that you are the right person for the job; however, you are lacking several key skills. Why do you think you are such a great fit?
- It appears that this position is several steps back in your career. My first thought would be you are desperate to get back to work and we are just a temporary job until you find your next career move. Am I reading this wrong? Help me understand.
- Your résumé states that you have various abilities and achievements but it gives little detail. Can you actually tell me a time when you....?

Never get hostile. Questions are never intended to insult or offend you. Sometimes the interviewer needs more information. Rather than being flustered or upset, be confident. Take the question as an opportunity to put a concern to rest and move forward. Always turn a negative into a positive. The last three places you worked may have closed, but make sure the interviewer understands that you were not the cause of the closure, but more the reason it could stay open so long.

Distinct Styles of Questioning

There are three distinct styles of interviews an interviewer can utilize to better understand your background. Direct, open-ended, and behavioral/situational questions are three distinct ways for the interviewer to collect information.

Direct Questioning is when the interviewer asks you exactly what they want to know. These questions predetermine the focus of how you would answer. e.g. Your information should be clear and specific. These types of questions, whether they relate to technical or soft skills, should be easy to answer if you have completed the research on yourself.

This technique is used to answer specific questions. Often times these questions are pre-determined, but additional questions could come up based on your responses.

The important thing to remember when responding to these questions is to focus on the question. People mistakenly drift from the topic and do not stay focused. Answer the question asked rather than give information you want the interviewer to know about you.

Make sure you use tangible examples. Companies do not want to hear about hypothetical situations. They want to know real life situations you have been in and how you have handled them. Make sure to use as much detail as possible, and do not be afraid to ask the interviewer if you have answered the question to his or her satisfaction.

Remember to create value during your phone interview. Use data/statistics as much as possible. The more you establish your worth to the company, the greater the chances they will want to pursue you further as an applicant. So be prepared with examples. Do not worry whether your numbers are exact; the interviewer is not going to go back to your company to confirm the accuracy of the data you gave them. However, make sure the numbers you cite are approximate or else you will create doubt in the mind of the interviewer.

Here are some sample Direct Questions that you should be prepared for:
- Tell me about one of your biggest accomplishments? Your biggest challenge?
- How would you describe your ideal manager?
- What characteristics describe your ideal work environment?

- What are your three greatest strengths and three greatest weaknesses? With weaknesses, use the opportunity to find ways to turn them into positives, or acknowledge the weakness and your attempt to improve.
- Why do you think you are qualified to do the job that we are looking to fill?
- Why are you currently looking to leave your current employer? (Don't be negative. Avoid any negative comments about your previous managers or companies)
- What is your greatest motivation in your job search?
- How do you feel about relocation, and have you addressed this with important family members and friends?
- What types of contributions do you feel you can make to our company?
- You have no experience with our business; how do you feel your previous experiences will be applicable in this position and setting?
- Why do you want to come to work for our company?
- What are some of our company's brands or products that you are familiar with? Make sure to not quote competitors. I cannot tell you how embarrassing it would be mentioning a competitor's product thinking that it is that of the company you are interviewing with.
- Salary – What do you currently make? What are you currently looking for with regards to salary?

What do you do when a company inquires about salary? This is the most challenging and often times the hardest question to answer. The second you start talking numbers, you greatly reduce your negotiability and quite possibly your chances to get the job. So what do you do when a company asks you about salary? How do you respond?

The best responses to the interview question concerning salary are simple—take the focus away from salary. Consider a response like, "I'm really not motivated by salary or income, but more so joining an organization that I know will help me grow as I help it grow. I expect a company like yours will offer me a competitive salary that matches my skills, experience, and education in the industry."

In nearly every case when you use this response, the interviewer will move to the next question. At this point you have taken away the importance of salary. You have refocused the conversation on what you can do for them and what they can do for you.

But what happens if the interviewer doesn't move on to another topic and insists you disclose your current salary or what your desired income would be?

Here are a couple of simple tips:
- Disclose your base salary, not your total compensation. Many times companies offer several avenues of income but when they are asking specifically about your salary, they are not looking for your total compensation; they are looking at your base pay. You do not want to appear over-priced.
- Once you disclose your salary, make sure to re-iterate that you do not want your current salary to be the factor that prevents you from moving forward in the process. Remind them this is about finding a solution for their needs and both parties growing mutually over time.
- If asked what you are looking for, at all costs do not give them a number. Talk around the question, or flip the question around: "What do you think someone with my skills and experience is worth to your organization? I value your opinion and believe you would know what would be the fair wage for what I have to offer."

- Do not tell the interviewer what the position should pay. This would be a very insulting response. I cannot tell you how many times I have had people tell me what a position should pay rather than what they are looking for.

Open-Ended (or indirect) Questioning is not as common technique that companies use but it can be the most damaging to the person being interviewed.

This questions typically are general and do not ask for specific information. This gives you the opportunity to determine the focus. It leaves very little boundaries on what you can say or how you can respond. Often times these phone interviews start with either "Tell me about yourself," or "Walk me through your résumé." In response to these particular questions, you should briefly summarize areas specific to the job talking about your education, experience, skills, and personal attributes. If possible, make your response relevant to the job you are seeking.

The most important thing to remember is to be clear and concise, but detailed-oriented, when responding. Do not be vague and do not use hypothetical examples. Try to mirror your experience to the company's needs and do not forget to touch on how your experience would apply directly to the job that you are interviewing for. Omit details that would not likely benefit the interviewer.

Remember your basic phone interview skills and the do's and don'ts. This style of interviewing is very relaxed, which leads to some candidates letting down their guard. Remember this is an interview. Be conscious off what you are talking about, how you address the issues, and what information you are providing to the interviewer. It may sound stupid, but sit up straight when on the phone and make sure you are smiling. It not only changes the way you project yourself over the phone, but it also helps you to project yourself with more confidence when speaking.

Because this technique is so open-ended and there are really no target questions, this is where it is very important to understand the needs of the company and the job. If you do not present skills and experience that are needed for this role, and the interviewer does not ask about it, then you have likely left doubts in the interviewers mind. Market yourself well.

Listen, write, and then engage. The information you get from the interviewer when talking about the opportunity, the company, and its needs is the basis of how you want to market yourself throughout the entire interview process. This is an opportunity to get a true picture of the position and what the company is looking for. This will also help you decide what examples you want to give in response to questions they ask.

Be prepared to ask questions at the end. Of course, remember that time is everything. The interviewer scheduled only so much time for the phone screen. So limit your questions to the two or three that are most important to you and will benefit you the most during the rest of the process.

Here is a list of sample questions:

- What happened to the last person that was in this position and what are some of the challenges that person had in the role?
- What is greatest challenge of the position?  In what areas is this person evaluated the most?
- What skills or experience are you going to value the most in the person that fills this role?
- Who does this person interact with on a daily basis within the company?
- Can you tell me what the typical day for this person would be like?
- What would you say is one of the most important attributes that you are looking for in this person?
- How do you envision a person in this role impacting your team and business?

- Are there any skills or experiences that this person must have in order to be successful in this role?
- What is the 3-, 6-, 12-, 24-month plan for a person in this role?
- What qualities did the last person in this job bring that made him/her successful in the role?
- Are there any needs that you are looking for that you feel I have not clearly addressed?
- Are there any skills that you feel I may be missing so I might be able to further clarify my experience?

Here is a list of questions to avoid:
- Do you think that I fit this role and plan on continuing with me in the process?
- How did I do?
- What is the salary range for the job?
- Can you tell me about the benefits?
- Do you think I would be a fit for any other roles in the organization?
- How soon will I be promoted or have opportunities of promotion?

Behavioral/Situational Questioning typically is ways to identify how a person approaches problems or how they have performed in their past experiences. This helps them understand your analytical and critical thinking skills. In these cases, the interviewer is asking you questions pertaining to what you have done, not what you would do for them.

In preceding chapters I talk about using a method called STAR (Situation Task Action Result) to answer questions of this nature. This provides you the opportunity to tell them about past experiences on how you have handled certain situations and ultimately how you have driven results.

This leads in to the most common interview style of interviews which is behavioral style questioning. Also, what we referred to previously as the STAR method. It is very important to come prepared to talk about how you have truly impacted the organization and the growth and profitability of the company. Often times company use measures similar to performance matrix and KPIs to measure personal, departmental, and company performance and ways to enhance this performance.

Make sure you come with plenty of solid examples. It is definitely not a problem if you do not know the exact numbers, but at least have a good idea on the scenario and the approximate numbers involved. Follow the methods talked about in the STAR method and other behavioral style responses to emphasize your impact on the organization.

The key reason for these questions goes back to the concept of creating "value." Not only do you want to create value, but that company wants to see how you can bring value to the organization. Companies will use this method of questioning to get a true understanding of how you fit. Remember the used car analogy? You need to walk away with the employer feeling like they have to hire you and know why you are worth it.

One of the best ways to hit key areas of a concern within the current organization, so you can highlight actions you have taken in the past addressing similar issues, is asking the right questions. Do not forget to ask the interviewer on what their biggest areas of concern are within the organization and for this position. What are some of the biggest challenges? Use this information when responding to situational questions using situations where you have solved similar problems. Address their issues by offering similar issues you have addressed in the past.

This in turn builds a rapport with the interviewer. The interviewer suddenly can relate to you more. You understand some of the problems and that is important to them. Building rapport helps quite a bit to get to know the interviewer which helps leads to questions you can ask to better understand the company and the work environment.

In addition, when you build a rapport with the interviewer, then if any questions you answer lack the amount of substance that the interviewer initial was looking for it will be overshadowed by some of the similarities in the issues and problems you both have dealt with. Relating on issues and building a rapport then ultimately drives success in the future relationship once you are hired.

You definitely want to take advantage of your ability to ask questions. But use these questions as an opportunity to better understand the position, the job, the manager, the company focus, the strategy, and the goals of the role. Do not use this opportunity to be selfish. Use it wisely. You want to make sure you address the concerns of the company.

Most importantly you want to tell the employer why you are the most interested and qualified person for the company. Make sure you show your enthusiasm about the company and position throughout the whole conversation. Ask intelligent and rewarding questions that benefit both parties.

Make sure you ask for an interview and the job at the end of the conversation. Simply tell the interviewer that you are excited about the opportunity and joining the organization, and then ask the interviewer when you could come in and meet with them in person. Show your enthusiasm and interest. There was enough dialog and information exchanged in the initial interview where you should be able to express your interest sincerely. Let the hiring committee know that. When you hang up the phone, they have already decided on how they want to proceed.

Thank you notes are a simple courtesy showing them appreciation for taking time to speak with you. It will not influence a decision, especially at the phone interview stage. Save thank you notes for after the face-to-face interviews, do not send them after the phone interview. Later on we will talk about the use of thank you notes and when they are valuable in the process.

Do not forget the goal of the conversation—to get the job. Brand yourself. Make sure the interviewer knows what you can offer the organization and how your abilities may fit with their needs and the overall strategy of the company. You do not have the job yet; you need to convince them you are the one they want.

Tim has been set up for a phone interview through a recruiting agency for a job reporting to the plant manager of a plant. Since this is the person he would be reporting to, he knows the manager will ask a lot of questions that are technical in nature. Tim knows how important the bottom line of a P&L is to a company. He is preparing to highlight both sides of his experience and will go into detail with examples and how he has created an impact to the bottom line of the P&L. After doing research on the company, he learns that they have recently started driving lean manufacturing initiatives. He knows his strength in this area could be a huge asset in further moving these initiatives forward. Once the phone call is over, he plans to ask the manager to come to the plant to meet him in person to get a better feel for the organization and present a better background on himself.

After hanging up the phone, Samantha feels great. She got a call from a company two days ago and the corporate representative set her up on a call with the HR Manager for a division of this large Fortune 100 Company. She practiced over the phone with a friend on reflecting her enthusiasm and excitement for getting into a more branding specific role and using examples that would highlight these experiences. The phone call lasted about forty minutes and she was able to articulate in short two- or three-minute answers specific examples to each of the HR person's questions.

At the end of the conversation, the HR Manager asked her if she had any questions and Samantha asked, "What does your organization need me to do in the first 30, 60, and 90 days to create an immediate impact on the organization?" The HR person answered the question and then told her that she would be hearing from her in a couple days to set up another interview with the hiring manager. She concluded the call by telling Samantha that she was impressed with the strategic nature of her question at the end, which focused on the company's ultimate business goals.

In the finance world, networking has been key for George. He has talked to many clients that he knows from his personal finance positions and has told them a lot about his ability to help grow and create profitability in many people's financial portfolios. One of his old clients sent his paperwork to the VP of Finance at a large services company and he has a scheduled call with the VP later today. His old client told him that he made a strong personal recommendation to hire George, and told George that he just needed to focus on his strengths in investing and growing capital. With the positive referral to the VP, he knows that he has a great chance of getting the job as long as he follows his old client's direction.

Pete has sent out hundreds of résumés via job boards and company website applications. He has gotten a lot of thank you and résumé acceptance letters but very few callbacks. He did get a phone interview yesterday, which he felt went well but the company said that it had a lot of candidates it needed to talk to before making any decisions. Most of the questions that the HR person asked him centered on what types of leadership he has gained in his time working during college and in any organizations he has been a part of. He talked a lot about how he was in two elected offices in college and how he was the editor of the high school newspaper. This focus was to demonstrate to the manager that he has led many teams and groups of people. The feedback at the end of the call was positive but it would be two weeks until they called him back. Since he got such a positive response on that call, he is going to continue to focus on those types of examples. He did do some research on the company and has sent a thank you e-mail to the HR manager expressing his appreciation for the time they took to talk to him and his excitement to learn about next steps.

# INTERVIEWING THE COMPANY

One of the most significant elements candidates forget when interviewing with a company is that they are not the only person being interviewed. Not every company is a fit for every candidate, much like every candidate is not a fit for every company. Earlier in the book we talked about developing career goals and parameters of your job search. You need to remind yourself what you're looking for in your future as well as the present. These will help you determine the best questions to ask the company and what observations to make when you are meeting with a company.

## Making Observations

It is very important to make observations when you are going through the interview process because it will help you evaluate your comfort and confidence levels in the company's environment. The observations you make should be centered on how the company treats employees, remains focused while presenting information, and how it treats you during your visit.

Of course you want to make sure you bring questions with you to the interview. The hiring committee expects serious candidates to take the time to compile thoughtful, relevant questions for them to answer. The questions you ask them should both be focused on the organization's growth plans, strategies, and the outlook of the position – but they also should inquire about attitudes of people at the organization, the work environment, what do they think about working there, and what does the company do for their employees with regards to benefits, personal surroundings, employee motivation and development, and promotional opportunities.

## Questions to ask yourself

Because it is very hard to write things down while you are actually involved in the interview process, make sure when you leave the interview to pull your car off the road and start writing down impressions from the interview.

Here are some questions to ask yourself:

- What do I think of the area where the office/company is located?
- When I arrived to let them know I was there for an interview, did someone greet me, introduce me to the company, and instruct me on the steps to begin the process? Did I have to wait long and how did it feel?
- What did I think of the office, plant, and work environment?
- Did it seem like the environment was organized and well-ran?
- Was the process organized? Was there a schedule and did the interview team do their best to stick to the schedule?
- When I met with each interviewer, did it seem there was enough time allotted to get a comfortable feel for the person, and were both parties able to ask questions?
- What types of questions did the interviewers ask and what was the focus of the topics?
- Were people smiling and noticeably happy to be there? Or did it seem like the environment was stressful?
- Did the company stay consistent on how it described the job prior to my visit, and how it described the job during my visit?
- What didn't I like about the environment?
- Did the interviewers all seem to ask questions from a standardized list and seem to focus on the same topics, or were the interviewers asking questions freely at their own discretion?

- Would I consider the work environment better or worse than what I had expected?
- What did I notice about the diversity of the environment as far as age, race, and cultural background of the people?
- Did the interviewers say anything negative/derogatory about the environment or people? What was said about the environment and people that was positive/complimentary?
- Did the company seem to care about my comfort in its environment? Did it offer me water, ask whether I needed a restroom break, or offer me lunch?
- Does the company provide a safe work place? Does it focus on the employees' safety before the bottom line?
- Now that I have seen the company and learned more about the job, am I still interested?

The importance of asking yourself these questions is to be comfortable with the place you will go to work on a day-to-day basis. There is a level of expectations that you will have when you walk into an environment and it is very important to make sure to evaluate this once you have left the interview. You lose 70% of what you see, hear, and are exposed to in the first few hours, so it is critical that you answer these questions and write them down so you can evaluate the organization at a later time.

## Approach is Power

How you approach asking a company and interviewer's questions can be critical in determining the tone of the interview. If you approach the interviewer in a poor way then you could negatively impact the result of the conversation. Even though you may answer questions well, you might fail an interview if you don't ask effective, appropriate questions in the proper tone.

The following are things to keep in mind when asking questions during a job interview:

- Have questions ready for each interviewer; however, do not read from your notes. Confidently look at the interviewer's face and see how they respond to your question (it is best to look at the space between the eyes). Not only does this show your sincerity in the question, but also helps you identify whether the person responding is being sincere.

- Once you have asked a question, allow the interviewer a chance to respond. The worst thing you can do is to interrupt the person while they are responding to your question. This shows lack of interest in what they are saying. This also will frustrate the person and create a negative platform for the remaining questions.

- Try not to ask questions that focus on you more than the broader aspect of everyone within the organization. You must remind yourself that you do not want to focus your interest on your needs but more on the company's needs.

- Make sure you have good posture when asking questions. It not only shows attentiveness to the person's response but also shows how serious you are on wanting to better understand that person.

- Do not be afraid to ask targeted questions that might produce some level of discomfort or a negative response. Remember this especially if you have learned of things during the process that would be a good reason to avoid the company. Get clarification on your concerns before you make any decisions to not pursue the opportunity. Make sure what you are hearing is consistent and supported.

- Make sure when posing a question to an interviewer that the question is relevant to their experiences within a company.

Asking someone a question they cannot answer will not produce legitimate results and is a waste of valuable time.

- Always ask open-ended questions and keep them as short as possible. By asking an open-ended question you are encouraging the person responding to give you an in-depth answer. Do not allow this to consume the conversation. Avoid asking questions that can simply be answered with a "yes" or a "no."

- Be careful how you ask questions that may appear leading. For example, if a company has a poor reputation of retention, do not ask them, "How would you explain your retention issues?" Rather, ask the question, "How would you describe the company's ability to retain its employees?" If the response leads to retention problems, then you can inquire further on what the company has identified is the cause of those problems.

- Never ask questions that begin with "Why" unless it is a follow-up question to an already given response. The reason to avoid "Why" questions generally is that these questions are often presumptuous. If you ask a "Why" question without certainty of the facts, you are potentially going to cause concern in the interviewer.

- Try to avoid asking questions that you believe would make you look desperate for the position. Candidates will seem or act desperate when they really need a job. Asking questions that directly reflect this will only make you look more desperate, even confrontational. So avoid questions like, "Do you see me as a fit?" or "How soon can I expect to hear from you because I am ready to start?" Although it may seem that you are simply being enthusiastic about a position, it is generally perceived as desperation.

- Be confident and always smile. Do not react negatively to unfavorable information you learn about a company during the interview However, you do not want to indicate your concerns to them.

## Getting the Answers

Many candidates don't recognize a crucial objective of the interview: for the candidate to have the hiring committee answer questions about the job, organization, and environment. Make a list of things related to the opportunity and the company that you can ask during the interview process.

The following is a list of topics you absolutely want to avoid during a job interview:

- Salary/Benefits (unless they offer to discuss)
- Work hours—(it would be better to ask the interviewer, preferably the hiring manager, what the typical day would be like in this position)
- Do not ask personal questions about any of the interviewers, especially related to EEO-related topics (religion, sex, race, sexual orientation, marital status).

The best questions you can ask the interviewers and people at the company would be related to the work environment, the position, what they think of the company, their jobs, and what the dynamics (atmosphere) of the environment are like. Questions should focus on the company, but at the same time give you information that will help facilitate your thoughts on how compatible you are with the work environment.

First, let us look at some core questions that are necessary to understand the true direction of the company:

- **"What is the company's vision and strategy?"** Ask this question of all your interviewers. What you are looking for is consistency. If everyone responds in a similar fashion, you then get a clear idea of the company's direction. If the answers are all very different, there may be reason for you to be concerned with the company. You need to dig deeper after the interview if these types of red flags occur during your questioning. This could mean that the communication among the leadership and the managers of the company may be ineffective, which would draw concerns on how you could be effective or successful in the organization.

- **"When the managers of the company commit to something, do they follow through with their commitments?"** Because this question could have negative responses, the answers you get may not be the most honest. Interviewers will not put themselves in awkward situations, especially if it may get back to the other parties on the leadership team. However, there are occasions where this type of questioning will uncover some loose bolts within the way the organization operates. This is a great question to ask a potential coworker or peer.

- **"How would you describe the ethical behaviors of the organization? When put in a situation where the company has to expend money to do the right thing, does the company act appropriately?"** You would be shocked on the ways companies can cut corners to avoid extra costs. In many cases this can endanger the end product or cause harm to the potential long-term view of the company. A tarnished image could result in long-term restructuring of the company because of a decline in revenues.

- **"If you could describe the overall characteristics of the leadership at the company in three words, what would they be?"** This is a great way to find out how the company truly is led and operates. This gives you a good idea of the style of leadership and how employees are viewed within the organization. There are two distinct ways lower level employees are viewed by a company: one being the most important, the other being least important. You want to understand where the company stands on important issues so you know how to approach your job and succeed in your career.

- **"What is the overall attitude among the employees on where the company is headed organizationally?"** This addresses the overall happiness of the employee pool. Many of the questions you ask may not be addressed openly and easily by the interviewer, and you may get some sugar-coated responses, but you can actually get a feel for whether someone is being sincere just by watching the person's overall demeanor and projected responses.

There are many other questions that you can ask interviewers that can give you a big picture idea of how the company is to work for and what the feelings are inside the company. There are also great questions that will help evaluate what it will take to be successful in the role if you are the one awarded with the opportunity.

The best question to ask the potential hiring manager is, "What would you say are your most important needs and priorities that you would like the person in this role to accomplish?" Using the word accomplish is critical in this question because the hiring manager views the success of his own job based on the accomplishments of goals set for the positions that report to him. In this case you are not only showing a sincere interest in your own capabilities of being successful, but also showing care for the manager to be successful as well.

Some other questions that will allow you to dig deeper into the organization and the position would include:

<u>Employee Retention, Development, and Leadership</u>

- "How long have you been with the organization?"
- "When you first started with the company, what were your responsibilities or your roles, and how has your career progressed since you have been here?"
- "When you think about coming to the office, what would be the best words to describe how you feel?"
- "Why would someone want to work at your company versus going to one of your competitors?"
- "How would you describe the company's vision and goals? Do you feel the company supports these on a day-to-day basis in the everyday environment?"
- "What is your company's current ability to retain their employees? Do you feel you have any retention issues within your company, and if so, what would you say are some of your biggest challenges?"
- "What brought you to the company?"
- "Where have you worked prior to this company and what things would you say make this company better?"
- "How many managers have you reported to while being in this position?"

<u>Characteristics of a New Hire</u>

- "What qualities made the last person in this job successful? What were some of his or her biggest challenges?"
- "What technical skills would you say are most important for the potential candidate to possess in order for him or her to be successful?"
- "What specific kinds of characteristics or traits would you say are important for a person to have to be successful in this role?"
- "What are some of the most important things you look for on a resume when trying to distinguish between candidates during an interview?"
- "Can you describe a typical day for the person that will be filling this role?"
- "If you could describe your ideal candidate in three words, what would they be?"

Goals of the Organization and the Position
- "What caused for this position to be available?"
- "How would you describe the management and leadership style commonly used within the environment?"
- "How would you break down the main functions of the position and the importance of each function?"
- "What are the most important things you are trying to accomplish with the next person in this role?"
- "What would be your 30-, 60-, and 90-day expectations for a new hire first coming into the organization?"
- "Are there any particular projects or initiatives that this person would be expected to work on upon starting with the company?"
- "What types of changes do you expect in the organization over the next 3-5 years? How do you expect the company to grow?"
- "Who are your competitors and what does your company do to differentiate itself from the competition?"

- "How do you measure an individual's performance in this role and does the company have a way to plan the future development of the person in this position?"
- "What is the vision for the person in this position for the next 2, 3, and 5 years?"
- "Where does this department fit within the overall scope of the company?"
- "What are some of the biggest challenges this person would have with the current employees in the department?"

Concluding the Interview

Now that you have had a chance to interview me and ask me questions pertaining to my skills and experience, what concerns, if any, do you have regarding my ability to do the job?

The worst thing you can do in an interview, no matter who the interviewer is, is to not ask any questions. Even if you ask the interviewer the same question as the last three interviewers, ask a question. Candidates feel that as long as they got answers to their questions they really do not need to ask additional questions. But interviewers like to know that the candidate wants their opinions or thoughts on the organization and the position. A candidate's lack of questioning shows a lack of interest.

Asking the same question to different interviewers, as cited above, also helps you to determine consistency and level of honesty. This can make an overall impact on how you feel about working for the company.

Another advantage that you gain when you ask a lot of questions is you have the ability to steer the direction of the interviews and ultimately leave an interview with a positive energy. There are two distinct parts of an interview: the first five minutes and the last five minutes.

The first five minutes are critical to capture the interest of the interviewer and make sure they feel you are fully qualified for and engaged in the opportunity. The last five minutes are critical to not only educate yourself more on the company so you can determine if this is the place you want to be, but also remind the interviewer why you are the right person for the position and wanting to be engaged in the role.

Finally, there are always leading questions that you absolutely want to avoid in an interview process. For example: "Am I going to be required to take a drug test prior to starting?" This would likely make the interviewer or the company assumes you wouldn't pass a drug test. You do not want to set yourself up for this image.

The other types of questions you want to avoid are questions that could lead to discrimination indirectly, unless it is imperative to know before accepting a job. If it is important to know, then wait to ask the question till after they extend you an offer for the job. For example: "Does your company offer Domestic Partner Benefits?" You do not know how the company or interviewer views sexual orientation, which is completely irrelevant to your abilities to do the job. You do not want to open any reason for them to discriminate against you based on things that are not relevant to the position.

Other areas that you want avoid are questions involving:
- Age
- Smoking/Health Problems
- History of Sexual Harassment or Termination
- Financial Problems
- Psychiatric Needs or Issues
- Job Security
- Attendance History
- Nationality
- Amount of Hours Necessary to Work
- Marital Status
- Religious Beliefs
- Disabilities

- Criminal History
- Problems with Previous Management
- Past Disciplinary Actions

Think about the goals in your job search and ultimately the goals for your career when pursuing information on the company. Do not let anything distract your focus on the ultimate goals you have set and written down. Remember that you are interviewing the company just as much as the company is interviewing you. This is a relationship that is a two-way street and there should be a comfort level from both parties on how this relationship can be successful in moving forward.

In the manufacturing industry, environments can be drastically different. Tim needs to make sure that he is going to be comfortable in whatever company he goes to work for. He also wants to make sure his management style and personality will work well in the work environment. When questioning people in the interview process, he needs to identify and focus on how well he and the company fit together. Some questions that come to mind are whether the environment is union or non-union, do people feel they have a voice in the plant, is management open to change to meet their goals, what are the people, who report to the position, looking for in a manager, and do people generally feel or seem happy.

In order for Samantha to be successful in a brand role, she needs to make sure the company strategies and initiatives have the potential to be successful. If a company doesn't have a clear vision, their strategy does not make sense, or they do not seem to have a focus on long-term development, this can make creating a successful brand very difficult. If the brand can't be successful, this could drastically affect Samantha's ability to be successful in the role.

George knows that taking an investment role within a company can be very challenging and often times brings volatility in the role. He cannot afford to fail in his abilities to grow the company's assets. Therefore it is important for George to understand the company's willingness and flexibility in the way he invests its assets, whether it is conservative or very liberal/aggressive in how it manages them. It is also very important to really understand the financial stability of the organization; this will drive George's ability to build upon what it has.

Pete wants to build his future. He wants to get with a company that puts a lot of focus on organization and employee development because he is very inexperienced in the work force. If he identifies that a company puts a lot of money and time in training and growing their people, this will allow him to learn more, develop faster, and ultimately grow his future. It is also very important to him that the company treats its employees well. So he will focus a lot of his questions around retention, how fast and in what ways people grow within the company, and how long people have been in their roles.

# INTERVIEWING FACE-TO-FACE

It is make-it-or-break-it time. This is the big chance to win the company over. This is what you have worked so hard for—getting yourself in front of the company so that you can present yourself as a solution and a need for the organization. This is the single most important part of the process. This is where everything you have learned in prior chapters, all your goals, and branding come to a head and you get the opportunity you were looking for.

First and foremost – Relax. One of the most common things I hear candidates say is that they are nervous. Nervous behavior can be misinterpreted with insecurity, lack of confidence, assumptions of lying or misleading statements, and overall poor performance. The reason you are interviewing is because you are qualified and have the experience that you believe they need in this role. I often tell people that you are not interviewing with the President of the United States, and even if you are, he started out where you are sitting. Put yourself in the interviewers' shoes, and put them in your shoes. This is a natural state that allows people to get from one place to the next. Be yourself. Focus on what you offer and do not over-compensate.

There are two purposes of the interview process: First, this is an opportunity for the hiring committee to confirm your qualifications and see how your personality and leadership style will work in the company environment. Second, this is also an opportunity for you to interview the company and determine if the company's environment and future goals and strategic plan will meet the needs of your short- and long-term goals. Remember, you started this process based on goals you developed. You want to make sure at the end you can say that you met those goals.

So the basic things to remember when you are getting ready to go on an interview:

- Be Yourself – Do not try to be something that you are not. You need to be yourself. It is similar to a marriage. If who you are does not fit well with the person you are with, it will not work long-term.

- Educate yourself – Do as much homework on the company as you can. Find out things about its work environment; scope out where it is located; look into its reputation and what people say about the company. These are not necessarily fact, but use the information to formulate questions for the company. This will not only help you answer some of the interview questions, but will also formulate some of the questions you may ask of them. Educating yourself on the organization is a critical part if there is truly a sincere interest in the organization.

- Confidence – Be confident and have a positive attitude. Again, do not be nervous. You should be confident in your abilities to do the job and make sure this comes out during the interview process. You need approach the interview with the attitude that you should be in the job already.

- Personality – 80% of the success of an interview is how you come across. Make sure to keep telling yourself that you want the job. Build up yourself for the interview.

- Appearance – This is always such a complicated topic to address because over the years I have heard of some of the strangest things that have occurred with regards to dress. I will talk about this more in subsequent pages.

- Role Play – get with someone that you feel comfortable with and practice interviews. Have them ask you questions and then you practice answering them. Your mock interviewer should provide feedback on what you say, how you present it, and how long you take to answer the questions. Ask them to be critical.

- Company Directives - Research the terms, methodologies, and initiatives that the company pushes and promotes. This will become valuable in the interview process. We will talk about some examples of this.

- Speak Professionally – Make sure you do not become too casual or use unprofessional or childish language in your interviews.

- Questions – Prepare a list of questions that you want answered during the interview process. Bring numerous questions to your interview. One of the worst things you can do is to not have any questions when an interviewer asks you for some. Write out a list of 20 to 30 possible questions you may want to ask, knowing that you will never ask them all.

- Timeliness – Do not be late. Make sure that you know exactly where it is, how long it will take you to travel to the location, and plan to be there 30 minutes early. You can always wait outside the building until right before your interview. A great saying that speaks volumes is, "If you're early, you are on time; if you're on time, you are running late; if you're running late, you might as well forget about it."

- Application – When filling out an application, make sure to print clearly and legibly. Do not rush through the application and do not leave fields blank. Make sure to bring information on former employers including addresses, phone numbers, previous bosses, and references. Lastly, under the section asking about desired wages or salary, always write negotiable.

Prior to an interview, you should always come prepared to provide copies of your resume, references, and any other pertinent information related to the position. Make sure you bring extra copies. It appears unprofessional to run out of copies of your documents. Do not forget to bring a pad of paper and several pens so that you can take notes. The last thing you want to do is ask the interviewer for a piece of paper or a pen.

Next, bring any supplements to your resume. Depending on the level or type of position, you may want to bring samples of your work, examples of how you have dealt with problems, applicable programs that you have designed or implemented, and technical documents or certifications that speak to your experience.

You might do well to prepare a presentation for your interviewers. Again, depending on the level of the position or type of position you are interviewing for, this may or may not be applicable. But even some entry-level candidates can use presentations to increase their chances. In my last year of college, I created a presentation / PowerPoint for presenting to perspective interviewers. In it, I described my personality, work ethics, educational knowledge, pre-graduate work experience, and goals with the company. I had this presentation spiral bound, with a clear cover and black vinyl back. I brought one for each interviewer.

In my last semester, when I interviewed with 128 companies, I always presented them with a copy of my presentation. The reaction was extraordinarily favorable. In fact, during the process, as I learned more about the companies and the positions, I was actually turning down second and third round interviews, and even offers. One of the most frequent follow-up responses I received from the interviewers was, "At the end of all our first round interviewers, I could not help but pick up the presentation you left, which reminded me of you. No one else did anything like that." You want to leave a lasting impression that makes you stand out among the competition. Five job offers later, I landed my first job out of college.

The presentation you make must be focused on both you and the company. Consider it a proposal of a partnership. Use pictures and copies of the company logo along with your picture to integrate the two in the presentation. In the presentation, you should focus what you know the company needs, wants, and looks for in an applicant and why you match those needs.

An interview presentation might include, but is not limited to, the following:

- Desired level and type of experience
- Educational and training requirements
- Company strategy, vision, and initiatives
- 30-, 60-, and 90-day plans when going into the role
- Accomplishments, Accomplishments, Accomplishments. Use this as an opportunity to highlight what you have done
- References – you can include references toward the back of your portfolio to encourage them to consider you as a candidate.

The presentation can be as simple or as elaborate as you want it to be. It ultimately will represent you as a brand. So when putting together the presentation, keep in mind the brand that you are trying to create. This is a fantastic opportunity for you to not only make sure you brand yourself, but also leave them something to remember you by.

The last thing to prepare for before the interview is to focus on your appearance. I cannot tell you how many times I tell people to think smart when dressing for a job interview.

Basics of Dress and Grooming

- Always dress slightly better than the environment. If it is a casual environment then dress more business casual. If it is a business casual environment, don a sport coat over your shirt or blouse. If it is a formal environment make sure to wear a suit. Think of where you are interviewing and with whom you are interviewing. You definitely can be under dressed, but you really can never be over dressed (that is as long as you do not wear a tuxedo).

- Focus your outfit on neutral colors that everyone likes. Do not wear a bright purple suit with a top hat to an interview for a $100K engineering job (yes, it has been done before). Try to focus on conservative colors and outfits that appeal to the masses.

- Do not overdo it on the jewelry, especially if in a highly regulated environment like a manufacturing plant where jewelry is not recommended at all. Do not wear gaudy items and do not wear anything that may be flashy, like expensive watches or jewelry.

- Make sure that you groom yourself properly, especially if you have a lot of facial hair. You do not want the interviewer to remember you because of your overgrown beard, unkempt hair, or distinctive smell (good or bad), etc. Do not over-use cologne or perfume: in fact, use to a minimum.

- Do not forget to check your breath! But do not chew gum

- Before you leave for the interview, stand in front of the mirror and ask yourself this simple question: "Would I hire me?"

- Finally, shut off all cell phones, pagers, alarms, and anything else that may interrupt the flow of an interview. Even better, leave them in the car!

You are now ready to go to your interview and get the job! Now it is all up to you. It is time to focus on what you do best—being you. Remember the basics. Do not get distracted.

TIME TO INTERVIEW

Arrive early! The last thing you want do is be late for an interview. The start of the process will set the tone for the interview. So make sure you arrive on time, have a confident and positive attitude, and emit the attitude that you belong in that job.

Now that you're prepared for the interview, here are important matters of etiquette to remember when interviewing:

- Address people appropriately. Unless they tell you to call them by their first names, assume they prefer Mr. (last name) or Ms. (last name).
- Say hello to everyone. You never know who has an impact in the hiring decision. One time I had a candidate lose the chance of a hire because he walked right passed the janitor without acknowledging the gentleman's "Hello."
- Use a firm and confident handshake when meeting people. Confidence is determined from your attitude, your smile, your handshake, and your responses during the interview.
- Make sure to use eye contact. People who do not use eye contact generally are indicating a level of insecurity.
- Do not use any derogatory or insensitive comments or remarks. This includes using profanity, slang, or casual phrases. Speak professionally.
- Do not disclose anything to do with your age, race, sexual orientation, or any other personal aspects of your life that could potentially be used against you in consideration for the job. We would like to believe that people do not discriminate, but even if only subconsciously, most people do.

There are several different types of interview settings that you should be prepared for. This can mean one-on-one formal conversations, group interviews with multiple interviewers, on-the-job interviews, and casual interviews.

One-on-One interviews generally are interviews that take place in an office or in a conference room that involve one individual asking you questions and discussing the company and your background.

Group/Panel interviews generally are the same as the one-on-one interviews but they involve multiple interviewers. These interviews can be challenging because you need to make sure you constantly make eye contact with everyone in the room and give each interviewer a chance to ask questions.

On-the-job interviews are interviews that involve walking around the work environment, often referred to as a tour, but still considered an interview. This is an opportunity for the tour guide to talk to you about the work environment on a day-to-day basis. This is also an opportunity for you to make observations and ask questions. This also means actually working or doing something that pertains to the position so they can evaluate your performance in the company's specific environment. Do not be afraid to address what you believe may be concerns not only for yourself, but even for them. If you find a major safety hazard before it becomes a problem you score big points with the company.

Casual interviews are generally interviews that take place when you are having lunch or in a casual meeting environment where people are just talking about the day-to-day events. This is the area where people let their guards down. This is often when people talk too personally and use unprofessional language, behaviors, and actions. Remember, if you are still with a representative of the hiring authority or company, you are still interviewing.

When you researched the company, you likely identified some of the company's primary initiatives. The interview is the best time to talk about those initiatives, especially if you have experience with them. Not only should you be prepared to ask questions about these initiatives, but also be prepared to talk about your experience with these initiatives.

The following are examples of common initiatives:

- Six Sigma or Lean Environments: This is generally a methodology that involves eliminating defects or deviations in a process or department.
- Safety: Companies are constantly trying to improve safety for their employees. There are teams and programs designed to ensure this.
- Self-Directed Work Teams: This is bringing a group of people together, each possessing different skills and capabilities, to work on an initiative without the typical managerial supervision.
- Environmental: Many companies have environmental and recycling programs. These programs often help with overall cost of operations, but are also designed to help the company's public perception.
- Performance Matrix or Key Performance Indicators (KPI): These are industry terms for measuring performance within a company and using this data to train, develop, mentor, and manage the organization.

Many companies are very open about their use of or support of these types of initiatives; therefore, they are not hard to find out about and they're easy to understand. Companies are times very critical about people who do not support such programs. So be careful not to say anything that would be directly against or unaligned with the programs they have in place within the organization.

This leads into the most common interview style: behavioral style questioning (referred to previously as the STAR method). It is very important to come prepared to talk about how you have truly impacted the organization and the growth and profitability of the company. Companies often use indicators similar to performance matrices and KPIs to measure and enhance personal, departmental, and company performance.

Make sure you come with various real examples. It is definitely not a problem if you do not know the exact numbers, but at least have a good idea of the scenarios and the approximate numbers involved. Follow the STAR method and other behavioral style responses to emphasize your impact on the organization.

The key reason for these questions goes back to the concept of creating value. Not only do you want to create value, but also that company wants to see how you can bring value to the organization. Companies will use this method of questioning to get a true understanding of how you fit with its environment and policies. Remember the used car analogy? You need to walk away with the employer feeling like they have to hire you and know why you are worth it.

One of the best ways to discover areas of concern within the current organization is by asking the right questions. Ask the interviewer about his or her concerns within the organization and about common concerns pertaining to the position you're seeking. Use this information when responding to situational questions. When have you had to solve similar problems?

This, in turn, builds a rapport with the interviewer. The interviewer can suddenly relate to you more. You understand some of the problems and that is important to them. Building rapport helps to get to know the interviewer, which leads to questions you can ask to better understand the company and the work environment.

In addition, building a rapport with the interviewer may help compensate should your answers to interview questions lack substance. Relating to the interviewer on issues and building a rapport ultimately drives success in your future relationship once you are hired.

Do not forget that answers are not the only thing you need to remember in an interview. Remember that your body language, eye contact, and the way you react to things can build a foundation of comfort or concern for an employer. Eye contact is most important because when someone does not look in the eye of the interviewer, there will be concerns that you lack confidence, honesty, or ability.

You need to not only observe the body language of others, but also remind yourself to be cognizant of your body language. For example, when you have your arms crossed in front of your chest, people automatically assume that something is wrong or you are mad, but it could just be that you are comfortable crossing your arms.

Sit up tall and do not slouch in an interview. Your posture shows you are confident, assertive, and strongly believe in what you say. Use your hands and be animated with your facial expressions. It is truly important to create a synergy between you and the interviewer.

Listening to the interviewer and then responding is also a very important attribute to follow in the interview process. Most people do not understand what listening means. I look back at the many times where someone was asking me a question. While they were asking the question, I was thinking how I would respond. This is not listening.

Listening requires you to listen to the entire question and then to think of a response. The best way to assure that you are listening is actually summarizing or paraphrasing the question to the interviewer before answering the question. Repeat in summation what they asked and then start answering the question. This forces you to listen to the entire question and then respond.

Focus on the question and only answer the question that was asked. Do not go off on a tangent and just keep talking. People commonly think that when a question is asked they can answer the question and then somehow slip in more and more information so they can continue to sell themselves. When answering the question asked, your goal in the answer should be to identify the skills that you possess by the example or response you give. These are the skills identified in the job description and by the interviewers when telling you what their needs are within the department.

Another benefit of listening to the question before actually answering the question is that you will be more likely to answer correctly. Collect your thoughts before you respond. Talk yourself through the answer, especially if you know the answer but it has been a long time since you talked about the situation or the use of the program or system. Take your time. Interviewers understand that sometimes you need to think about how you want to approach the question, concern, or need of the interviewer.

Lastly, be true to yourself and do not compromise your beliefs. Integrity should never be compromised for a company or a manager. You need to remember these things. Companies respect someone who has integrity and sticks by his or her values. Ultimately it will come out in the interview process, especially how you answer the questions and what you say.

There are a lot of things people do wrong in an interview that can really cause the interview to take a negative turn quickly. Even though many of the things you will read about in this book sound like common sense, they are not. Common sense fails people every day in our industry. So make sure you remind yourself of boundaries and how to carry yourself in an interview.

One of the most damaging mistake people make during an interview is to talk too much. This can be when answering a specific question, especially when the response is negative or has negative overtones. It also happens when people stray from the actual question and talk about things completely unrelated to the topic.

I realize that some interviewers can make you feel very comfortable and it natural to relax and let down your guard, but you are still interviewing. If you have to address an issue in your career and it has negative overtones, minimize the answer. Do not give over-detailed explanations when a brief answer would suffice. Often this happens when talking about being fired or dismissed from a job. Do not tell the company everything. This is one of the rare occasions in the interview process where being vague will benefit you.

Absolutely under no circumstance bad mouth former employers, employees or people you have worked with. This includes talking about having to pick up other employees' slack in previous jobs and how you had to do more than your job expectations because others were under performing. When you bad mouth a company or former employer, you have no idea who the interviewer may know or how that experience may have a negative impact to that person. Also the interviewer does not want to think you have the comfort of talking negative about the people you work with. It is a sign that you could cause personal conflicts and problems among your fellow coworkers.

> A company was recently interviewing one of my clients and it asked her, **"What would you say is your biggest hope or desire for the next five years?"** My client's response illustrates the dangers of becoming too personal and comfortable with the interviewer. She responded, **"I would love to meet the man of my dreams and see where it goes."**

After I received the feedback on the candidate and what she had said, I confront her about it. I wanted to know why she would respond so openly. She confessed that her mistake was that during the interview she grew too comfortable. She felt that interviewer was comfortable talking personal and did not think it was an inappropriate response. She got too personal.

Do not get flustered or concerned if you do not really have an answer to a question. Of course it is important to answer the question the best way you can, but do not let it throw you off track. It is very common when a person is confronted about a skill that they may lack, or not have much experience with, that they lose confidence and start fumbling. Stay focused. Fumbling one question does not mean you've failed the interview or ruined your chances for the job.

The other thing to remember is that no one is perfect and has every quality and skill that a company could want. If you are confronted with a question or a problem that you have not dealt with, talk about how this weakness is an area that you would want to immediately address. Do not allow your lack of knowledge in one area to make you feel disqualified.

To summarize, there are many rules and methods to ace an interview. Some important things to remember are simple:

- First 5 Minutes – You need to grab the interest of the interviewer in the first five minutes. Present the most valuable information and experience right at the beginning. If you start off strong, you will likely end up strong.

- Make a good First Impression – A future employer's first impression of you generally is the springboard for you getting the job. Try to determine the person's likes and dislikes. What are their expectations and make sure to follow interview etiquette.

- Focus on their Questions – Do not forget to stay focused. Do not ramble. I cannot stress enough how when you ramble or go off on a tangent you not only lose the interest of the interviewer, but you also take poor advantage of the time they have invested and want to invest in asking additional questions.

- Achievements – Stress your achievements, records, and accomplishments. Companies want to know your success stories and how you have impacted the organizations you worked for previously.

- Be Prepared – Do not walk into an interview without doing research. If you come in unprepared, you are not going to appear prepared.

- Ask Good Questions – Ask questions of the interviewer that are strategy-related. Focus on the company's values, goals, strategies, and visions. Forget about salary and benefits! One of the best questions you can end a conversation with is, "Are there any concerns you have with my abilities to do this job?" Use this as an opportunity to help get them past these concerns.

- Confidence – This is key. As I said earlier in the chapter, if you are confident then they will be confident in you. Tell the employer what you are going to do for them and how you will help their company grow.

- Never Talk About: Salary, Extra Compensation, Benefits, or other incentives.

At the end of each individual or group interview, make sure you ask for the job by telling the interviewer your interest in coming to work for the company. Another great way to end an interview is to tell the person you are talking to that you are looking forward working with them and joining the team. Reflect confidence that you are the right person for the job and the one who will be rewarded the opportunity.

Thank-you Letters

Upon completion of an interview it is often a commonly accepted practice to send out thank-you letters to the interview team. A mistake people make is to assume this is another opportunity for them to pitch their background. Thank-you letters are just that— an expression of gratitude. When you are writing a thank-you letter, focus on thanking the interviewers for taking valuable time out of their schedules to meet with you.

Why do you not want to pitch your background? Simply put, at this point it will not make a difference. Ninety-nine percent of the time, once you leave an interview the company already envisions where they see you within the organization, if at all. A thank-you letter containing a lot of inflated, subjective opinions about you will not change that. In fact, I have seen thank-you letters sway the company more negatively than positively. The biggest reason is that information that is put in the letters is not always accurate, spelling and grammar errors are present, and the interpretation of the results of the interview are not consistent with the company's. If you do choose to send a follow-up card, focus on thanking them for the time, expressing your interest and enthusiasm for the company and the position, and expressing interest in hearing from them.

Here is an example of a simple, but well-appreciated, thank-you letter:

Dear Mr. Thompson:

I appreciate your valuable time to discuss ABC Company and the (listed title) position. It was a great pleasure meeting with both you and the rest of your team. I definitely feel my qualifications and skill set will fit well within your organization and truly help your company be successfully.

I can honestly say that after learning more about your organization and the opportunity, I am more excited about joining your team. I look forward to hearing back from you on the next steps in the process.

Please feel free to contact me at your convenience at (phone number) or (email address).

Sincerely,

Peter Thomas

The only exception I might allow with thank-you letters is if you absolutely forgot to mention something in the interview process that you find extraordinarily important to bring to their attention. Just remember one thing: if you did not say it then, they may be concerned on why it took so long after the interview for you to mention it.

If you are working with a recruiter, make sure to consult with him or her before sending a thank-you letter. Most recruiters will ask you to forward it to them for review and then they will forward it to the company. It is highly disrespectful and sometimes very damaging to you, the applicant; if you go around the recruiter and contact the company directly, even to send a thank you note.

Lastly, in my professional opinion, thank-you letters are not necessary. At some point following the interview process, I would rather see an applicant follow-up with a phone call to the hiring authority, thanking them for the opportunity and asking if they have made any decisions on how they would like to move forward. If you are working with a recruiter, it is important to go to the recruiter for follow-up, not directly to the company. This way you are personalizing it with a phone call and, at the same time, trying to get some closure.

Tim has been working with a recruiter on a position and got the good news that his phone interview went well. He was invited out to interview for a Production Manager position with a company in South Carolina. A couple days prior to the interview, the recruiter preps him on the company, how to approach the interview, and makes sure he calls the recruiter once the interviews are complete.

He has done his research on the company, phone interviewed with the Plant Manager, and is prepared to go in and get the job. He arrives early at the plant and is initially led into a conference room with three managers. They pose him a case study situation where he has to tell them what he believes are the problems, how he would approach fixing them, and ultimately what results he would expect from his method of approach.

Next, Tim is interviewed by several members of the plant leadership team including the Plant Manager that he will be reporting to. He also interviews with several of the supervisors that would be working for him. He uses a lot of situational examples on how he could drive operational improvements with the plant. He also hears the needs of the supervisors in wanting a manager that will be a leader. He talks about organization and employee development and concern for helping his employees in areas of further personal development.

While talking to the supervisors reporting to him, and a peer within the leadership team, he can truly identify with their style of leadership and how he will work well with the team. He can see himself working in the plant, and he tells the Plant Manager of his ability to be a cohesive part of the team. He notices that there is turnover among the hourlies and some of the supervisory staff, but believes he can reduce this by engaging better with the employees. This is something the supervisors have identified as missing in the plant.

As he is heading to the airport, he calls the recruiter to brief him on the success of the interview. The recruiter asks him whether he has an interest in the role, and Tim expresses that he can truly see himself there. The recruiter then asks Tim if he would be willing to move right away to start if the position was offered. Tim is ready to go.

Last week Samantha completed the initial stages of the interview process with a large consumer products company. She has successfully completed three phone interviews and is scheduled to fly out this morning to interview with the company tomorrow. Her flights are delayed and she gets in late, drives immediately to the hotel, and gets as much sleep as possible so she can be sharp and truly prepared for the full day of interviews.

The next day, she arrives early and is excited about talking with the company. Her day of interviews consist of nine interviews, meeting with various marketing, sales, and operations leaders within the company. She even has a meeting with the Division President. The company asks her a lot of questions regarding how she has successfully taken brands to market and made consumers more aware of brands. She has no problem citing many examples of how she has done this throughout her career.

During the interview she asks each of the managers what the company strategy and vision are. By doing this she can truly see whether everyone is aligned within the company. This is important for a brand to be successful. She also talks to them about previous brands and strategies that have been successful and those that have failed, and why. She has determined that the goals of the company are strong and she believes she can help drive its brand success. She flies home hopeful that she represented herself as a strong candidate.

For weeks George has been networking with people that he knows in the industry. He was asked out to lunch by the CFO of a local consumer services company. They met for lunch and spoke to him for nearly two hours. Three days after the lunch meeting, he was asked to meet with the CEO, President, and the Chairman of the Board.

George walks into the corporate office with two objectives in mind: making sure that the company is financially sound and the leaders are open to new ideas in growing its assets, and showing the executives how he can truly grow their company. He initially meets with the CFO for about thirty minutes before meeting with the rest of the interviewers.

The interviews seem to be going quite well. During the interviews, he presented each interviewer a presentation on how he proposes to grow the company's overall portfolio of assets. The leaders of the company are very receptive to how he has invested previous clients' assets in the past and his ideas on how he can truly grow the company. He also gets a full picture of the finances of the company and its strong cash foundation, making the company very strong financially. He knows this is a company that has done well, and with proper leadership and direction it can truly continue to grow aggressively.

As he walks out of the last meeting with the Chairman, the CFO walks up to him and walks him out the door. George tells the CFO that he is extremely interested in helping them build the company's assets. The CFO tells him that he was very successful today and that they will be checking references before giving him a call later next week.

Pete realizes that with little experience out of college, he will really have to focus on selling his abilities. He has an interview this morning with a retail organization that is looking for a corporate trainer. He thinks that his previous leadership experience from work and training knowledge from his internships will fit well with this role.

During his interview, he continues to detail how he has mentored and trained employees on how to conduct business. He also discusses how he has shadowed other managers at his internships on how they engage with their employees and create a successful business environment.

Pete asks numerous questions about where the employees started with the company and how they got to where they are today. He is noticing a positive trend with the company. It seems that everyone has been with the company for at least five years and they have been promoted several times since they started with the company. He is excited to join the organization. He goes home and immediately writes thank-you notes and puts them in the mail.

# OFFER STAGE: GETTING THE JOB

Waiting for a call back is often the most frustrating part of the interview process. During this time, candidates might reflect back to the interview and wonder, "What if I had answered a question differently or spoke on a specific topic more? Would it have helped the company in the decision-making process?" An important thing to remember, whether you get the job or not, is to be happy with how you interviewed. Learn from the experience, and if you do not get the offer, decide what you can do differently when you interview in the future.

It is also important to remember the playing field at the time you are interviewing. Depending on the industry and the economy, there certainly may be a lot of people out there that are available to the company to hire. Just because you do not get the job does not necessarily mean you interviewed poorly or that you are not a good candidate. It even could have come down to a "coin toss", which I have seen before. Even if a company has two very solid candidates that interviewed for a single job, it can only pick one. So before you start criticizing yourself for not getting the job, remember the environment and the atmosphere of the interview process.

I look at the employee and employer relationship very similar to a marriage. Both parties can like each other, but if the personalities do not match well, or the attraction (skills) is not there, then you do not want to get in to a marriage that will just end in divorce. The goal is to make this a long-term relationship, not a short-term one. So remember when you get the final word on whether you got the job or not, look at it for what it is.

The other thing you must remember is that just because a company is not leaning toward making you an offer, sometimes this can change.

First, understand some of the most common reasons people do not get the job:

- The employer does not feel the candidate brings the skills and experience that will be successful in the position

- The candidate said things in the interview process that leads the company believe that he is not interested in the role
- The employer does not think the candidate's personality would fit well with his team
- The candidate makes discriminatory comments in the interview, either offending the hiring committee or creating a negative impression in their minds
- The candidate does not ask questions of some of the interviewers, ultimately showing lack of interest in the position
- The candidate is not able to answer questions in enough detail, leading the company to be concerned on his/her capabilities to succeed in the position
- The candidate's unprofessional appearance and/or behavior are off-putting to the committee

Any of these reasons on how a company responds could seem like there are little chances that you could get the job. Some of these responses could be countered. It all depends on how the company decides to approach letting you know of their decision. You need to remember is to think through a plan before reacting.

An example on turning around an employer's decision would be if the employer feels that because of certain actions during the interview, you appeared not to be very interested. If the company calls you to tell you this, you have an opportunity, at that moment or soon after hanging up with them, to re-address the issue. First, try to find out what you said or did that would have given the impression that you were not interested. With this information, you can try to explain how that was misinterpreted and then emphasize your interest in the opportunity and articulate why. You might also write a follow-up letter to the hiring manager and address the concern. Showing your enthusiasm through your persistence can lead a company to reconsider you for a position.

What if the company tells you that you did well but you lack a certain skill set that is really required for the job? There are several ways this can be handled. If you have the skill set and you just were not able to evidence this in the interview based on the questions that were ask, address it now. Make sure you drive your point home and give examples of how you really do have the skill set that they require. If you truly do not have the required skill set, but you have other skills similar or complimentary to them, highlight those.

Another problem could be you did not thoroughly answer the questions to the interviewers' satisfaction, which leads them to wonder the amount of experience you have in that particular area or topic. Take the opportunity to address the concern. Offer some additional information to the hiring manager to convince him/her that you really have the experience but there was never a request for clarification. Often times I would advise following up with a letter with clarification as well because this can be a very sensitive and important part of the decision process.

Knowing that you have the ability to persuade the employer in your favor is prepared to respond when you get the call. However, do not respond hastily. Do not let your emotions get the best of you and lead you to say something that may make your position even worse. Think before you respond to the manager's concerns. If you think it may help, do not respond on the phone but follow up with a letter. Even though you may think it is a risk, I guarantee you that the committee will read your letter. Preparation for the call is key.

The phone rings and on the other end the hiring manager is telling you they made the decision to make you an offer. The news that you have been waiting for has finally arrived. There are many aspects of an offer process, an important thing to remember is to be gracious and thank the representative for the opportunity to be able to join the team. Do not respond negatively to anything that he/she says, but simply confirm what he/she says by repeating back and confirming the offer. Once the hiring manager is done presenting the offer, ask as a follow-up if the offer will be sent to you in writing with benefit information.

Most companies will follow-up an offer with a letter in writing; however, some companies will not put it in writing till they have a verbal acceptance from the candidate. No matter what, make sure that you thank the manager for an offer and commit to a timeframe by when you will get back to them with regards to a response to the offer. The commitment of a response is not necessarily a commitment of an acceptance or decline, but a response that may include asking for additional details or a counter-offer proposal.

You may decide when the offer is actually made that the offer meets all the needs and goals that you set forth when starting the process, and surely it is tolerable for you to accept the offer over the phone when the manager extends it to you. But if you want to review the offer or possibly negotiate what was presented to you, you do not want to accept the offer until you have negotiated. Once the offer is accepted, it is nearly impossible (not to mention unprofessional) to negotiate that offer.

Once you have the offer and have all the details necessary to make a decision on how you want to proceed, establish what is important to you and what is not important to you. The reason you did not accept on the spot may have nothing to do with the salary; it could have to do with the benefits, the vacation, the work schedule, or, in the grand scheme of things, you may still not be 100% sure you even want the job.

Now that you have the offer, it is critical to sit back and think of your emotions and what is driving your decision throughout this process and at this point. However, the reasons as to why most candidates do not accept jobs have to do with money/salary. Whether you are working with a recruiter or on your own, you really do not know where the salary falls into the range they are willing to offer. So negotiating a salary presents risks. Understand that the second you call the company back and tell them you would like to present a negotiated offer, there is a risk of losing the offer entirely. By doing this, you are hypothetically turning the job down and presenting them with an offer for them to review and either accept or decline. If they choose to decline the offer, they also have the option of rescinding the offer that was initially presented.

So when considering the salary that was presented to you, the most important question is, "If the company decides to not meet your needs on the offer, are you willing and comfortable with not getting the job?" It is certainly not often that a company would simply walk away; however, there are many of companies that I have dealt with over the years that have made it clear up front, or in their actions, that they will not negotiate offers. So be careful when making your decision.

When considering a counter-offer based on salary, think of the possible mindsets of the company:

- The company intentionally presents a low offer as an invitation for negotiation
- The company made a fair offer, but they are willing to pay more for the "right" person. There may be some wiggle room in the offer at this point, barring there are no equity issues within the company.
- The company does not typically entertain counter-offers and will offer the best possible package.

Another great way to consider whether an offer should be negotiated based on salary is to break it down at an hourly rate. Understand the amount you are working for and break down the actual worth of your time in relation to the proposed salary. Do not pass up an offer merely because it falls short of your expectations by an insignificant amount. There may be options for a raise in the near future. Focus on the big picture.

Also take into consideration other benefits and added pay that comes with the position. You need to take in to consideration bonuses, commissions, and various added benefits like a cell phone, computer, car or car allowance, along with standard benefits like cost of medical, 401k, and tuition reimbursement. Ultimately the decision to negotiate is up to you, but make sure you look at the entire offer as a package, not just the monetary salary.

If you decide that you want to propose a counter-offer, this action should be justified. These reasons could vary depending on the situation.

Some examples of justified counter-offers include the following:

- Salary or Wage is lower than your current (or most recent) position
- Cost of relocation is going to put a large financial hardship on you based on the compensation they are proposing
- At your current job, you receive a yearly raise and are scheduled to soon be making more than the proposed offer
- Bonus payout for your company is within a couple months and if you put your notice in then the company will not payout your bonus
- Your current company will require you to payback relocation money if you terminate your employment with them before a certain time
- Your current or last position included certain financial benefits (or material benefits) that decrease the value of the offer.
- Cost of living in the new location is higher than your present location.

Before you pick up the phone and contact the company, there is one last question you need to ask yourself: How does accepting this offer bring you personal satisfaction and improve your ability to achieve your long-term career goals? You need to make sure that if you are prepared to counter the offer that you understand the risks. They could decide to take the offer off the table.

When you pick up the phone to contact the company or if you decide to write an e-mail (if the offer was presented electronically), make sure you are very professional and do not allow your emotions to control you when discussing the counter-offer. Start the conversation by emphasizing your excitement and enthusiasm on getting an opportunity to join the organization. The company needs to feel reassured that you are serious about joining the team and that this negotiation is not just about money.

Explain to the hiring manager that when you started this process you were expecting the salary to be in a certain range (quote them a range) and that you were a little surprised at where the offer came in. Also make sure you explain to the hiring manager that you did look over all the benefits and other monetary gains connected to the position and still feel that the salary is slightly lower than what is fair. This is when you want to explain to them why the offer may be less than what you have previously earned, and justify why you feel you deserve more.

Be prepared to give a firm number that you would be happy to accept if offered, and make sure that the number is fair and consistent with positions of this nature across the industry. Do not ask for something that is unrealistic and expect the company to react well to the offer. An unrealistic counter-offer will often time result in a negative response from the company.

Most companies will not give you an answer to your salary request at the time of the request. They will tell you that they have to investigate the equity within the organization to make sure that any salary adjustments they make to the offer can be justified. This process usually involves going to the HR department or the financial officer to make sure that all the numbers work.

Make sure you reiterate to the hiring manager at the end of the conversation how sincerely interested you are in the opportunity and hope that you can come to a fair and reasonable agreement that will be a win-win for everyone. You also should make sure you express the understanding that the company has to take into consideration a lot of factors when presented with a counter offer, and that you would appreciate the opportunity to re-review an offer even if the salary is not adjusted.

Usually when an offer is countered it will take a company a day or two to get back to you with regards to the newly proposed salary request. The proper people will need to review the situation and the numbers to make sure it works with everyone involved. Then the offer has to go through another round of signatures before it is re-presented to the candidate. So if you do not hear back from the companies right away there is no need to assume anything negative; they're simply performing their due-diligence to get the offer right.

There are several possible scenarios to be prepared for:

- **The company meets your request for a higher salary.** If you receive the call letting you know that they are matching the salary that you requested, make sure you are very gracious, and accept the job on the spot. Be prepared to discuss a potential start date and any other necessary steps needed for you to formalize your acceptance.

- **The company understands your need for a higher salary and meets you in the middle by offering you a salary that is higher but does not match your request.** In this case, you need to be prepared on what your magic number is. If you are comfortable with any compromise then you can just accept the position and move forward. However, if you need a specific figure in order for you to be comfortable with the offer they are presenting to you then make sure you have that number in your head when they call you. If the offer they present to you is not what you asked for you can always ask for additional time to consider the offer.

- **The company does not feel that increasing the salary is justified at this point but will allow you to still entertain the offer as it was presented.** In this case, you need to sit down and really rethink the entire picture and everything that is being offered with the position. Remember the goals that you wrote down? Return to them and have a heart-to-heart with yourself to figure out if this is the right position for you. You do not want to pass up a great opportunity over a few dollars.

- **The company does not feel that increasing the salary is justified and has decided to rescind the offer.** In this case there is not much you can do. Unfortunately there are occasions where a company does not want to negotiate. You need to look at this as a learning experience. There is not much that can be done to change the company's mind in cases like this. I would suggest you don't attempt to re-engage, but that is your decision. The concern that you have at this point is that you have left a bad taste in their mouths and they may feel bruised by how things played out.

There is definitely no science to negotiating an offer because there are so many parameters that can alter the dynamics of the negotiation. Ultimately you just have to hope that whatever happens, it happens for the right reason. If the job was meant to be, and you get what you wanted, then you can feel happy to know you got one step closer to your lifelong goal. If you did not get the job because of the negotiations, you can always learn from the experience.

There are many other elements that can be negotiated in an offer. Some of these things are simple, like vacation, the start date, or coverage of medical till the company coverage kicks in. Most of these negotiations do not jeopardize the offer itself, but are more considered minor details looking at the big picture of the offer. The only other significant factor in the negotiations would be relocation.

Even if relocation is involved in the new job, not every offer will come with a relocation package. Companies may not offer relocation at all, or sometimes they will offer a relocation sign-on bonus in lieu of some type of package, which is usually paid after you start.

Along with this, there are many factors that can come into play for the person who is relocating:

- Cost to sell the house
- Realty fees
- Duplicate housing costs
- Movement of goods
- Cost of living adjustment
- Cost to buy a house
- Lease termination charges
- Short- or long-term storage

Most relocation packages are fairly basic with movement of goods, temporary living, storage of goods, and incidental expenses. Usually relocation packages, especially on lower level positions, do not include any involvement on the costs to buy and sell a home. These are factors that you must consider when thinking about the move and accepting the job. When a relocation package is offered there usually is not a lot of negotiating involved in the package because it is usually pre-negotiated by the company with the relocation service. Therefore, you are not going to be able to do much to have this changed. You can always ask for an additional signing bonus to help with any extra costs you may incur beyond what is covered by the package.

Companies may also offer a lump sum signing bonus in lieu of a package. The benefit to such a bonus is that you can do your move as cheaply or as expensively as you want and then pocket the unused money. Signing bonuses can also be negotiated and many times you can get more than what is initially offered, and counter-offering the relocation is usually not going to jeopardize the offer itself.

The only major drawback to signing bonuses is that often times a company will not pay you the bonus until two or three weeks after you start. This means that you have to finance your relocation yourself. This takes capital upfront and a lot of planning by the candidate.

Lastly, you can also run into situations where companies will not offer any type of relocation at all. This has become increasingly common in many industries due to the fall of the economy and decreased values of homes. Relocation is a major decision because you are going to incur a tremendous amount of burden and costs to get to the new location and may not recover those monies. There may be some tax help or benefits from paying for your own relocation, so it would definitely be a good idea to explore your options.

Overall, the negotiation process can be very easy or very difficult depending on how much you desire the job. How much you are willing to give up in what you're asking for in the offer can often times are determined by this. The decision essentially comes down to this. If you see the value in taking the job and taking a financial cut in your wages in order for you to gain ground on your long-term goals, then you will see the light at the end of the tunnel.

Once an agreement has been made, the offer is usually contingent on a background check, drug test, and reference checks. Because of these contingencies, make sure you are entirely accurate on your application including months and years of employment; any deviation in this information is cause for the offer to be rescinded. Unfortunately there is really no way around a drug test, especially if you are actively using drugs. Do yourself a favor (and save yourself the embarrassment and the company the cost of the test); if you know you are going to fail a drug test, let them know rather than taking one.

A company's request to do a reference/background check can be a pivotal point in finalizing your offer. I cannot tell you how many times I have seen candidates' reference/background checks turn up negative information. Either the references checked didn't give a positive reference, or they refused to give any information about the candidate, deeming that reference totally useless.

Before you hand out a list of references to potential employers, call each reference to make sure they will still give you a positive review and provide the support necessary to justify the company's hire. Also, this is a great opportunity to verify if the phone number is accurate and the person is still available to speak to the hiring authority. If a reference tells you that they cannot give a reference due to company policies, then you'll have to find additional references. Under most circumstances there really is no way around a reference's inability to give a reference due to the policies of his or her company. It may be awkward to initiate such a conversation, but you must confirm with your references that they are able to give a positive recommendation. If they cannot commit to this, remove them from the list and find another reference.

It might come as a surprise, but a reference can really blow up in your face. When I called a reference to talk to him about a candidate that was being hired for a departmental position, the reference could not say enough about how great the person was to work with, how they were always going above and beyond their job, and always exceeding expectations. But then, out of nowhere, the reference made a comment that the candidate would not be a good manager but more of a team member or support person. This is where a reference can hurt you, and depending on the role, potentially cost you a job.

The last thing you should remember is to not give references from a job that you do not have listed on your resume. I do not support or condone keeping jobs from your resume, but people do this all the time when they are short-tenured positions or if the position seemed to be a step back in that person's career path. How embarrassing is it to have a hiring manager call a reference and the reference says, "When I worked with John at Company ABC," and company ABC is not on John's resume? Yes, it happens.

An offer is not valid until the offer letter is signed, a start date is set, the background check and drug test are completed, and references are checked. After you clear these hurdles you can celebrate the fruits of your labor.

For someone who is unemployed, getting a job is probably the most exhilarating and satisfying part of the job search. It is a huge relief to know that the weight of not having a job has been lifted form your shoulders and you can now focus on growing your career and developing yourself professionally rather than worrying about how you are going to pay your bills.

For someone who is employed, there is one more major step left before you are in the free and clear: you have the (sometimes) difficult task of putting in your notice at your current job. This can be extremely challenging when you have been with a company for a long time and they have no idea that you have been looking to leave. It can also elicit an unexpected response.

Tim gets a call from the recruiter representing the production manager job he interviewed for the other day. The recruiter tells him that the company was prepared to make an offer and they were working up the numbers. The recruiter poses a question to Tim: "If the company offers you $80K, can I accept it on your behalf and give them a start date of April 5th?" Tim pauses for a moment and tells the recruiter that he would rather see everything in writing before making any type of commitment.

With some anxiety in his voice, the recruiter tells Tim that they have another candidate that they interviewed as well, and that Tim will need to make a decision relatively quickly. He reminds Tim of how long he has been on the job search and how challenging his search has been without having a degree. He again asks Tim whether he would commit to a salary of $80K.

Tim tells the recruiter that he would allow him to accept on his behalf if offered $80K.

About three hours later, the recruiter calls Tim and says "Congratulations". You start on April 5th. They offered you $87,600 plus a $5,000 signing bonus." Tim is very pleased with the results of the offer and confirms his acceptance. He calls the hiring manager, per instruction of the recruiter, to let the company know that he accepts the offer and finally get back to work.

The nice thing about being employed when negotiating a job offer is that a candidate has the ability to negotiate for better perks and options. Samantha knows this when she gets a call from CPG Company with an offer. The company details the offer for her and it seems fairly generous. The salary is 10% more than what she is making now. However, she is concerned by the offer including two weeks vacation while her current job gives her three weeks. It also offered her a signing bonus of $15K for relocation. She feels this is fair for relocation; however, she would not receive any money till 30 days after her start date.

After thinking about it for a day, she calls up the HR manager. She tells the HR Manager how pleased she was to hear that she was getting an offer and was grateful that the company considered her such a valuable future employee. She did, however, ask the HR Manager for an additional 5% on the salary, an extra week of vacation, and for the company to arrange for her relocation and deduct the cost from her lump sum. The manager sounded taken back by this.

Samantha explains to the HR manager that the industry studies and standards show that her current salary is below industry standards. She also tells the manager that she really didn't want to give up her vacation time. The HR manager tells her that he will call her back after discussing these points with the hiring manager.

Later that afternoon, the HR manager calls her to let her know that the company could not offer her any more salary; however, it was going to offer her a $5K signing bonus and a performance review after six months to evaluate giving her an increase. He also told her that although it normally doesn't offer new employees three weeks' vacation, they have decided to go ahead and grant her three weeks of vacation. With regards to relocation, the company also decided to accept her suggestion to arrange the move to her new location through the company's own resources and pay the moving company directly out of her lump sum she will receive.

Samantha excitedly told the HR manager that she was pleased with the modifications and she would gladly accept the offer. She is very happy with the way the negotiation process has turned out as the results of her efforts. Now she just has to figure out how she is going to tell her boss that she is leaving.

George doesn't have the benefit of being employed to help leverage his negotiations, but he is a numbers guy. When he gets a call from the CEO of the services company he has been interviewing with, he is told that they would like to make him an offer. The CEO explains that he will send the details to George in email, and asks him to respond no later than one week from today.

Later that day, George receives the offer details in his email. The offer is 20% less than what he was making in his last job, however, it offers a 10% bonus potential. After pondering his monthly expenses, he calls the CEO to let him know that he would like them to consider offering him 10% more. He explains to the CEO that he would see significant financial rewards in the long-term by hiring George for this role, but because of his monthly expenses, the present offer was a bit low.

The CEO explains to George that the company does offer a strong 401K match program and typically pays out over 100% of their bonus. George still requests the CEO consider increasing the base salary that is being offered. The CEO tells George he would call him back.

Two days go by and George has not heard anything. He is starting to panic, thinking that he really blew a good offer. He knows that a counter offered allows the company every right to simply walk away. He decides to send the CEO a follow-up email to explain that he is sincerely interested in joining the team and is looking forward to hearing back from him.

About an hour after he sends the email, the CEO calls him to let him know that they could only offer him 3% more on the salary. He explains to George that there are internal equity issues that just won't allow him to exceed that amount. George hesitantly accepts the offer from the CEO with hopes that after a few months of working there they will see how much money he will bring the company and possibly consider giving him a raise. He starts on Monday.

Pete, like any college graduate, is anxious to put his degree to work. The company he had interviewed with the other day has sent him a package in the mail. As he opens the package he realizes that he has been offered the job with a starting annual salary of $42K with full benefits. He is ecstatic! He calls the administrator who sent him the offer and tells her how excited he is to be a part of the company.

# RESIGNATION AND COUNTER-OFFERS

Putting in your resignation where you currently work can be difficult depending on the circumstances. Often times the company you are working for does not realize you are currently looking to leave the organization and the resignation letter typically will come as quite a surprise.

The following is a list of basic things you need to remember:

- Put your resignation in writing. You may tell your manager verbally but always provide a written resignation to him and the Human Resources Department. Always tell your manager first.
- Do not delay your end date. Give the company fair notice, typically two weeks, but do not prolong your exit if you do not have to. You need to focus on yourself and your new opportunity.
- Make sure you discuss with your manager how you both prefer this news to spread throughout the organization.
- Do not talk about counter-offers with anyone other than the company representatives that are offering it to you. It is not fair to the company to disclose this information to other people within the company.
- Always remember why you are leaving your job. Focus on the reasons for your change and do not allow anything to change that reason.

When putting together a resignation letter, remember to make it short, sweet, and to the point. Many people have asked me for help writing this letter. They show me a draft, which is often a three-page story of how they love the company, appreciate many things (listed individually); never thought they would ever leave the organization, and blah blah blah. That is exactly what the company is thinking as they are reading page after page.

Resignation letters are not meant to be fun or exciting; they are meant to tell the employer one thing: that you are leaving. So it is very important to make sure you keep your letter short, clearly state your intentions, and thank the company for allowing you the opportunity to work for it. Here is an example of how simple and direct a resignation letter should be:

May 1, 2010

Dear John:             (John being the employee's boss)

My employment with your company over the past (xx) years has been truly educational and rewarding and I hope that it has been for the company. Please understand that I have made the difficult decision to hand in my formal resignation from (company name). I have received an outstanding opportunity that will significantly enhance my career and assist me in achieving my long-term goals.

I regret to inform you that I will be leaving the company on May 15th (this can be two or three weeks' notice).

Thank you for taking the time to work with me over the last (xx) years and help me develop personally and professionally.

Sincerely,
Peter Smith

cc: Human Resources Department

You should always meet with your boss when you present him a resignation letter. Emailing or mailing the letter to your boss without meeting with him face-to-face is definitely impersonal, but it could be appropriate if you do not see your boss on a regular basis. Once you have tendered your resignation to your boss (as noted in the letter), you should deliver a copy of the letter to the Human Resources Department to officially notify them of your official intentions.

There are various possible reactions that you may receive when tendering your resignation, so be prepared for what will happen next. Reactions can be very forgiving and often times demonstrate how much the company values you. Conversely, reactions can be quite harsh and demeaning.

Here are general responses to resignations:

Positive Reinforcement with Congratulations

- Boss shakes your hand and tells you how happy he is that you have been able to find an opportunity that will help you progress your career. He accepts your resignation and affirms that he would like you to work your two weeks and remain a part of the team until you leave.

Negative Response with Affirmation

- Boss is completely shocked that you have turned in your resignation and starts asking you questions on what caused this. Bosses will start blaming people, including themselves, to figure out what sparked the desire for you to want to leave. Many times this can lead to anger and frustration, but it ultimately leads to your boss acknowledging the resignation without showing any level of acceptance or congratulating you for the opportunity.

Positive Response with Negative Results

- Boss is surprised yet happy to hear that you found what you think is a better opportunity for you long-term. He then asks for you to turn in your keys, calls HR and security, and they escort you, along with your belongings, from the office/environment. You receive very little time to think because they do not want you, having said you're leaving, to be around.

## Negative Response with Negative Results

- Boss is very angry and feels this is an act of disloyalty and betrayal. He feels you are purposely causing him to be short-staffed and are dragging down his department or team. He immediately asks you to leave the organization because he feels that any further attendance could cause additional negative effects to the team.

## Positive Response asking for Additional Time

- Boss seems very responsive to the fact that you feel you have found an opportunity that truly betters yourself and your career. He feels that there are many things that are left to be done before you leave, and asks you to extend your departure date till a few projects can be completed. This is an indication of how he feels you are a key contributor on his team and recognizes your decision was not meant to be harmful or malicious to the organization.

## Negative Response with Negative Environment

- Boss is very upset to hear that you are leaving and feels that you are making a huge mistake. He emphasizes how he feels this is going to be a negative impact on his team, but asks you to stay for the remainder of your two weeks because he needs you there as long as possible. During your last two weeks, people ignore you, do not respond promptly to your emails, exclude you from meetings, and give you the cold shoulder generally. Your work environment feels very negative and uncomfortable.

Obviously there are many ways a company can react to your decision to leave the organization. These are only a few scenarios that can occur when you approach your boss to let him/her know you are leaving. Just be prepared for the twists and turns because anything can happen. Remind yourself that you are doing this for one simple reason – you. This is not about the company, but more so about your goals in your life and career. Do not make it about them; make it about you.

The company is always going to take your resignation personally. They are not only losing an employee, but ultimately there is going to be a missing link within its organization. It is never easy for an organization to adjust to missing staff, especially if that person has a management or leadership role within the organization. It is because of this that the company feels your resignation is retaliatory and meant to hurt the organization.

## Counter-offers

So what do you do when the company comes to you soon after you put in your resignation and offers you more money and benefits to stay with the company? Do you think the company's driving force behind its offer is because it doesn't want to lose you, or do you think there are other reasons? This is why I recommend never accepting counter-offers from your current employer as enticement to stay. The following is a list of things to consider when a company counter-offers:

- What type of company waits till you threaten to resign before offering you more money or a promotion?
- How is it going to fund this increase or promotion you are receiving? Are the wages or position budgeted or within alignment with internal equity? How can this be justified for the long-term?

- The reasons or circumstances that cause you to leave are going to keep repeating themselves. Things do not change just because you put in your resignation.
- When you accept a counter-offer you are showing the company that you can be bought.
- You have made your employer aware that you are unhappy working for them. Your loyalty from here forward will always be in question.
- As the word spreads that you gave notice but decided to stay, your coworkers will start treating you differently and question what they want to tell you or include you in with regards to company business.
- Statistically, 90% of those that have accepted counter-offers in the past have either voluntarily or involuntarily left the company within the first twelve months.
- If your company goes through economic downsizing or restructuring, whom do you think is going to be looked at first for being laid off?
- When a new position opens, management often looks at their loyal employees rather than the disloyal employees.
- Your company may not continue to include you on special projects or get you involved in company-protected trade secrets or innovations. This will inhibit your ability to truly grow long-term.

Companies never like to be caught off-guard because then they have to figure out how they are going to handle their organizations and leadership once you leave. Surprising a company with your resignation and giving it a short time period to figure things out only drives the force behind counter-offers. People want to do their best to prevent having a loss within organizations that will cause instability.

Because the company does not want to have the instability in the organization, they start to think about ways to prevent imbalance. The easy way for a company to prevent such imbalances is to stabilize things. In this case, the only way to stabilize the situation is to prevent you from leaving. So the company will present you an offer to lure you back from the new organization. A company doesn't make a counter-offer because it wants to; it is doing so because you are forcing it to make this move, which leaves a very negative taste in the company's mouth. So what good will come from you staying with an organization long-term that believes you forced it to make this move?

Once the company stabilizes the organization, it has the ability to take a step back and look at the big picture. It starts to try to determine the next step to move the organization back in the right direction. The first concern that it considers is the weak link of an employee who really does not want to be at the company. Once the company has decided that your employment weakens the team, it is going to do what it needs to in order to fix the problem. Most companies would not consider training, mentoring, and counseling to fix a problem like this. The majority of companies will look at the easiest way to fix the problem, and that would be to replace you, the weak link.

Many surveys have been conducted on people who have been offered counter-offers and made the decision to stay with the organization rather than take the new opportunity. Nine out of ten managers say that within the first two years of them staying with the company, they are either discharged, asked to leave, forced to leave, or at some point remember why they were looking for a different job in the first place, which leads them to start looking again. Most people realize at some point during that time the purpose of them staying was not for them but for the company.

The other changes people often see in their relationship with the company are how they are treated. This can include being included in special projects or teams, being uninvited to meetings, limitations or declines in their reviews or bonuses, and a limitation in their ability to grow and further progress in their careers.

If you are absolutely convinced that counteroffers do not have to be negative, it is important to take great interest in how it is presented. If it is not in writing, then it does not exist. If the company comes back to you and offers you an offer to stay with the company, what you see is what you get. If you want the company to offer you a yearly bonus that sticks, you need to ask for it in writing. If your boss tells you that if you stay with the company he will make sure you grow within the company - then get it in writing. Promises are only as good as the paper it is written on. If it is not written down, then it is not really a promise.

If you really want to stay with the company and truly believe your boss is sincere, then ask him to put the offer of growth and progression in writing. If he is serious about his offer then he will not hesitate to put the offer in writing. If he does not feel comfortable putting it in writing then he really cannot promise you the things he says he can.

If he does not have the ability to put it in writing then he is going to try to make you guilty for asking him to putting it in writing. You have worked for him for how many years and you are asking him to write it down? How could you not trust him after all these years of him helping you? These are tactical ways to keep things on track for ---------- the COMPANY.

If he is not willing to write down your agreement at the moment of his commitment then you have nothing. It is not going to happen later that day, it is not going to come later in the week, and he is not going to present it to you at the end of the month. It will never come. The reason is because he cannot promise you something that he has no control over.

The biggest reason why people take counter-offers is that they really do believe the company values them and wants them there. Why do companies panic and throw counter-offers at employees who are leaving?

The following is a brief list of some possibilities:

- **Training** – a company has invested a lot of money training someone to do a position. Not only is there a significant amount of cost involved, but there is a significant amount of time involved.

- **Loss of Use** – when a person vacates a crucial role in the company, the company does not run well. There is something missing. A loss within the organization causes it to run inefficiently.

- **Employee Morale** – when people leave the company, the other employees within the company get concerned. They know that things are going to change. People are going to have to pick up the slack and do more. This will cause a hardship on the employees because they have to work harder.

- **Cost of Staffing** – the costs connected with filling a position can become very large. Not only is it the cost of advertising, interviewing, and training, but it also could be the high costs of recruiting fees.

- **Helping a Competitor** – the last thing a company wants is to lose employees to a competitor, especially in an industry that has a very competitive market. Every good employee lost is a gain for the competition.

- **Loss of Skills** – when a company surrounds itself with skilled employees, it does not necessarily duplicate these skills and characteristics among the team. It is classified as a team because each person brings special qualities and skills to the table that makes the team strong. A loss of one person with a special skill results in a loss of many.

- **Change** – no one wants change. As a whole, people hate change. When a company loses employees, things have to change in order to keep the company strong. Change creates dissention among the team.

- **View of Management** – many people's perception of management during high turnover is poor. If a manager loses an employee, the concern may be generated that it was not the employee's fault. People like to blame management, making the boss a target when someone quits.

Most people don't want to be the cause of issues in an organization, especially if an organization has treated them well. So consider how people might treat you knowing that you were the cause of dysfunction and unrest among the team. Think about how the environment was like prior to you giving your notice, and how might that dynamic change once you have given your notice?

Also, did you ever think why it took you giving notice to see the recognition and the monetary gains for your work? People do not always realize it took threatening to leave to get the raise, promotion, or support needed to feel successful. People don't like working in environments where they have to beg for something. That is technically what you are doing by giving a letter of resignation. You're begging them to match the offer so you will stay.

Think past the counter-offer. Do what I often call "peeling away the onion." Start by asking yourself many of the most important questions in this type of situation:

- If they offer you more money to stay, is this going to put you above the normal range of the position? This is a leading indicator that it is not a permanent action by the company. No company can afford to over-pay people within its organization. Not only does it cause a major equity imbalance, but it also negatively affects the bottom line.

- Your manager starts to sweet talk you. He tells you that he has not been able to talk to you about the fact you are under consideration for a promotion. He claims that because the move is confidential, they were waiting for all the important parties to come to alignment. Tactical? Yes. Honest? Absolutely not.

- Was the reason you were looking in the first place being addressed by the counter-offer? If you do not see an immediate impact on what was pushing you to leave the company then why would you expect it to change long-term? This creates an understanding that even with more money; it is still the same place.

- Will your coworkers and employees put their trust and loyalty in you knowing that you threw in the towel? Many of them probably like you and do not want you to leave. But don't you think that in the back of their minds they are wondering why you are still there? They know you are not happy, so how would that suddenly change for you.

- Remember that loyalty plays a huge part in a company's trust in its employees and how it treats them. Once you have breached that loyalty, the company has to prepare itself for the possibility that you will never be 100% dedicated to the company. Will you be a team player long-term? Is the fact that you were looking indicative of your performance as of late?

The real implications behind a counter-offer are devastating. While very tempting, the counter-offer can also be the first sign of a company not functioning strategically. Companies that are strong and forward-thinking are prepared for these types of situations when people resign. It is not in their policy books or protocols to give counter-offers because they know that the person will not work long-term. So making sure it has a plan to implement in these cases is critical. Any good company prepares itself for this situation. It does not let its employees take control of the situation by dictating how things are decided.

Rejecting the offer is something that needs to be done with confidence, conviction, and expediency. Accepting to entertain a counter-offer from another company shows your company your weakness. It tells your company that if it digs a little harder and works itself a little deeper, they just might be able to keep you for a little while.

However, are your goals predicated on a short-term solution for a long-term problem? Knowing that you could be let go for your lack of trust and loyalty in the company, do you really want to have the reputation of being a job hopper and not an overhaul contributor? Remember that it takes time to develop you within an organization and make a true impact.

My advice is to reject the counter-offer as soon as you get it. Convince yourself before any extra offers are made that no matter the offer and how enticing it is, you will stand strong and stick your ground. You want to stand by what you need and are looking for long-term in your life, your job, and your list of goals.

Tim, George and Pete are all unemployed and don't have to worry about putting in their notices and the possibility of counter offers. However, Samantha is not quite in that same situation. She now has to take on the hardest part of the whole process: to let her current boss (and a good friend) know that she is leaving the company.

Samantha schedules a meeting with her boss and walks in with a prepared resignation letter. She explains to her boss how grateful she is on all the things that she has taught her and done for her over the years. She also insists that her boss and she remain friends even after their careers take them in separate directions. She explains to her boss that she received a very nice offer from a company that would allow for her to refocus her career in the area of Brand Marketing.

At first her boss seems very happy for her and congratulates her. But then suddenly the mood shifts. Her boss explains to her that she is a valuable part of the team and that they would likely respond to her request in a few days. Samantha excuses herself from the meeting with hopes that the worst is over.

Later that week, Samantha gets called into her boss's office and the HR manager is there too. Her boss explains to her that they do not wish to lose her and are offering her a 20% increase in salary to stay with the company. Samantha is shocked that the company would offer her so much more money to stay, but also remembers all the things she has learned about counter-offers.

She explains to her boss and HR manager that her decision to leave the company has nothing to do with her compensation. She explains to them that she really doesn't feel the company could offer her the direction she wants to go with her career and regretfully declines the offer.

For the next week, her boss won't talk to her. She was excluded from several key meetings within the office, and a lot of her coworkers are treating her like she is working for the competitor, even though their businesses are totally unrelated. She realizes she made a good decision and works the rest of her two weeks with her head high as she prepares for her relocation.

# REFLECTING ON YOUR NEW JOB

First Arrival

Now that you are the new kid on the block, it is time to shine and show the company what you can do, right? No. No one wants a person to waltz into a new work environment and start implementing new changes within the organization. Remember that people do not really know you yet.

You need to first gain the respect of your employees, peers, and managers. The best way to do this is to sit back, listen, and observe. Take your time when giving your opinion and do not rush into any major changes, even if you think they are necessary.

Spend the first six months working on building relationships and trust with your new coworkers. Show them you want to better understand their jobs and the dynamics of the environment. Try to learn of the things already tried within the organization so you know not to repeat the same failures as others.

When getting to know your peers and managers, focus on your current role and not your past role(s). No one really wants to hear what you did that was so great in your last job. You need to work long, hard hours to establish a level of trust in how you approach things and what you are there to do for people.

Being a new person in the office can always be overwhelming because you know you can help, and want to help, but you also know you have to give it proper time. Listen to the people around you and their experiences. Think about modifications you can make and show team members how it would benefit them, along with the company, long-term.

It is definitely alright to criticize and critique; however, you do not want that to come across as being too strong or trying to overpower people at work. It is very important to gain the respect of other people in the office. You want to get to know them and the situation better rather than trying to throw yourself in the middle of the company's present situations.

Being confident, punctual, and driven is all very good, and over time can result in substantial, positive growth. Yet, one of the most effective ways to reign in the team is to listen and ask them for advice on how things should be done and what things have negatively impacted their jobs.

When you get people involved in your daily development you are actually already telling them that you have a high level of trust and belief in what they have done and can do for the company. Also, your peers and employees are more apt to work with you as long as you listen in regards to their challenges and their needs.

How does it Feel?

You have been at your new job for over six months now and you have settled in very well. You have met several new people and made numerous connections on a professional level with your colleagues. You feel that the company values what you are bringing to the table and your overall contributions to the position.

But go back to the goals you wrote down at the beginning of the book. Read over your ideals, values, and interests you highlighted as important to you. Utilize these things in the day-to-day of your work. While remembering that these goals may constantly evolve as you grow professionally, how has this new job affected them?

Do not get too comfortable.

Assessing the New Job

The whole point of this journey was to do identify the next step in your career and how it will facilitate meeting your goals in the long-term.

Reflect on the things you talked about earlier. Those same things you wrote down on what you were going for (career goals). Now sit back and look at where you are today. Do you see the things you were hoping for that will help you get to your goal, or do you feel that it is still a gross misalignment from what you intended?

Understand the things that make you happy. How has this new job supported the things that make you happy? What did it help you do to create that level of happiness you didn't have at your last job? You also need to do a similar exercise to evaluate some of the things in your new job that may pull you down and make you weaker. Ask yourself why these things make you feel this way. Make sure you look at the big picture of makes you happy; what is it and what causes it?

Now take some time and write out all the positive and negative aspects of your new job. Take the positives and negatives and compare them to your previous goals you have written. You need to make sure that the position and the job is aligned with most, if not all, of your aspirations. If it does align then this will lead to a feeling of success.

Because you spent the last six months really only observing, it is now the time for you to start trying to look at ways to better motivate, develop, and grow yourself and individuals you work with. Look back and see if there is anything missing, and if so, take action to try to correct it. You need to learn from your mistakes and take the necessary steps to live your life and allow it to move forward.

You need to create positive energy to drive future results. Make sure you find ways to create this positive effect even more than what you had before.

Breaking Down Your Goals

You need to remember why you are at this new job. Revisit your list of Goals, Values, Attributes, Skills, and Personality and develop a matrix. The purpose of this matrix or grid is to see what skills you are utilizing in your new job and what you are not. It also will help you to see what steps you are taking to achieve your goals in general.

Start by evaluating your previous job in one column on a scale of one to five, one being "not often" up to five being "very often," on how it addressed your ultimately goals. List them out and number them appropriately. Take the total and add it at the bottom. Now complete this exercise for your current job. Assign numerical values of each attribute and add those up as well. What's the difference?

How does your new job numerically stack up against your old job?

Greater

- If the number is greater in your new job you know you have succeeded in some way. This tells you by changing your jobs and looking at the goals you set, you have found a place that is much more of a positive impact than the last company you worked for.
- In this scenario, you want to spend a lot of time developing your job and the relationships with the people around you.
- Here you need to develop teams among the people you're familiar with because you know the attributes you bring and fulfillment the job provides you are personally satisfying.

Less

- Less can be tragic to anyone because you are figuring out whether you made the right decision in choosing this job. It does not fit your ideal job to reach your goal. You can certainly try to make some things better and more aligned with your expectations, and that certainly will help. However, you have to be prepared for the fact you may have made a bad choice in making the move you did.
- With this scenario, you need to review your lists and figure out if the new attributes you are finding comfort in within your new job would dramatically change the way you were shaped before. Can this shift actually get you to where you want to be?

Finishing Touches

Taking yourself through this process is an exciting opportunity to find fulfillment in your life, learn how to brand yourself, and get the job you want when you want it. It will help you become a strong interviewer, a better employee, and a strong future leader.

No matter how hard you try and how frustrated you are, the marriage may or may not work out. You have to define yourself and prioritize your needs. If when the dust settles you really haven't made headway on the goals and aspirations you were shooting for, it might be time for you to start your search again.

It has been three months since Tim started his new position as a production manager. Tim reflects on the one thing that made this search the most challenging for him: not having a degree. He figured that his experience with lean manufacturing and his desire to drive an impact to the bottom line would help him get into that next opportunity to build his career.

Unfortunately, the one thing he is quickly realizing with his new opportunity and position is that although they hired him on the basis that he has strong experience with lean manufacturing, they really do not believe in the concepts to make it successful. He has already begun to implement some changes to help improve some of the systems within his department and has received tremendous resistance. The most trying factor is that his boss does not support his decisions.

Tim has realized that although the job is the right thing for him for now, it is not what he is looking for long-term. One of his biggest goals is to nurture his passion for continuous improvement and lean manufacturing, and he is realizing this company will not provide him this opportunity. But, for now, he is going to make it his own and do his best. If he is not able to instill the change and beliefs in the people around him long-term, he will consider looking for another opportunity. But he will not give up this soon.

For Samantha, making this move was to realign herself with the life goals she always had but wasn't able to achieve. She loves marketing and loved the company she worked for, but it could not provide her the opportunity to get into Brand Marketing, which she feels is her true passion.

It has been almost a year since she started working for the CPG Company that hired her last year. Samantha absolutely loves the company, the people, and she has finally found her passion – Brand Marketing. She manages several brand portfolios for her company and drives several successful marketing program initiatives.

Originally her goal was to get with a CPG company that would give her the opportunity to get into Brand Marketing. Previously, she could never imagine managing several multi-million dollar brands. Now she is driving one third of the company's brand programs and has successfully driven sales up 26% in just under a year.

George decided to target his financial and investment experience to try to be successful in the corporate investment business. He felt that by using his skills in investing assets that he could work with a company's financial portfolios and help them grow. When the company hired him, it hired him with the goal to grow the overall value of its portfolio.

Unfortunately, the one thing that George did not expect is the fall of the market. Over the last six months the market has fallen tremendously, and a once-confident investor has had to walk into several board meetings trying to explain why the company's investments have taken a dive. Even though it is very clear that the market has taken tremendous losses, an investor is supposed to protect the company from those falls.

George has been put on a 60-day performance review. The company has given him one last chance to evaluate his own performance factors and how he is impacting the company's investments. Because George is a supposed specialist in capital investments and investment strategies, the CFO and Board have hired him as a subject matter expert. Now nine months into his job, he has one last chance to make it work.

George has consulted with several key economic advisors in the industry and they have helped him position the company's portfolio in a way that he hopes will cushion it form the market losses. He also has re-invested several of the company's assets in various commodities that he believes have hit bottom and have little room to fall.

He has realized what he can do, and has hopes for himself long-term. He is not prepared to give up just because the market has fallen. He knows that he can make money for the company and can build its assets to a new level. He has laid out a 60-, 90-, and 120-day plan to the Board that not only will recover major losses, but he predicts will bring strong gains.

George knows that investing people's assets is what he loves. He now wants to prove to everyone in his life that he can do it on a larger scale. This is his passion, his goal, and what he knows will drive him long-term. He will make this successful.

Every college kid has the same initial life dreams: to get with a company and help it develop, learn what it wants, where it can go, and get it there. Pete is excited about the opportunity that this company has given him. But, like most college students, he knows this probably won't be the only company he will work for. It is very common for college graduates to change jobs three or four times in their first ten years, trying to figure out what they want to do long-term.

Pete is no exception. He loves what the company is teaching him and really believes he loves being a manager. He is quickly finding out that although he loves training and loves managing people, he is not really happy in the retail industry. Because he knows how hard the job market is, and how important it is to get this initial experience out of college, he plans on sticking to his guns and continuing with this position.

He knows that long-term this is not where he wants to be, but he knows that he loves training. Now he just needs to realize his dreams and figure out what industry he wants to be a trainer in. He knows he likes the service industry because he really loves training employees and also helping customers. So over the next few years he is going to seek out his true passion, what will truly make him happy.

We look back at these four individuals and what it took for them to get where they are today. And although where they ended up may not be the final steps in their careers, they are closer to what they believe they want in life and what will bring them fulfillment. They may get in their new job and have work hard for what they want, and for others they may have to find another company to continue their career. But I think it is clear that their focus was all the same, realizing their dreams and long term goals.

The one thing I want you to take away from reading this book is that you are in control of how you feel, where you work, and in what type of environment. Only you can gauge your personal and professional satisfaction. Lastly, only you can be the one who makes changes that will still help you be a strong employee, but also help lead you through the path to the goals that you have in the end. It is important not only to be happy with what you do today, but to know that it will lead you to long-term happiness. Every step you take should take get you closer to this. Every change you make should lead you to that ultimate goal.

CPSIA information can be obtained at www.ICGtesting.com
Printed in the USA
LVOW051110070213

319095LV00001B/49/P